Swami

CHILD LABOUR – A STUDY

CHILD LABOUR
–A STUDY

D. CHENNA REDDY

SERIALS PUBLICATIONS
NEW DELHI

First Published - 2007

ISBN : 81-8387-066-X

Published by

SERIALS PUBLICATIONS
4830/24, Prahlad Street, Ansari Road
Darya Ganj, New Delhi-110002 (India)
Phone : 23245225. Fax : 91-11-23272135
E-mail: serials@satyam.net.in

CONTENTS

Chapter - 1

HUMAN RESOURCE AND CHILD LABOUR

Human Resource Development–Concept and Strategies

Human resources of simply, the member of people living in a country constitute is manpower. This is one of the most vital resources of country, because it is this force which exploits the natural environments for the entire population of the country, it is both the producer and consumer of all types of goods we need for our comfortable living. It thus, determines the level of economics development of a country. Some of the concepts of economic growth itself have taken a broader view of economic development in its institutional setting of socio-economic and political context. In this perspective the cherishes of allocation of resources in planning investments in 'capital goods' as well as investments, in human capital are being revised so as to go into the problems such as rates of return from the competing claims of the two sectors. Notwithstanding, human beings merely as 'capital assets' and their importance for promotion of productivity at different levels of the economic system, qualitative factors including social values, motivational patterns, potentials of developing entrepreneurial capabilities, their rights and duties as citizens, creating social awareness and raising levels of politicisation are being considered as important areas of analysis to view Human Resource Development as an integrative process.

The study of human resources is vital from the point of view of economic welfare. It is particularly important because human beings are not only instruments of production but also ends in themselves. The importance of human resources development, therefore, is being increasingly realised in making a more meaningful analysis of approaches towards integration of economic analysis of approaches towards integration of economic and social planning so as to view it as an independent variable and not treat it merely as dependent in the more classical, traditional, econometric models of development with GNP and growth rates as their prime objectives. Human Resource Development also views development as a cooperative partnership between the Government and the people through social institutions and organisation promoting voluntary action, giving a sense of self-direction to the local people and increasing self-reliance as important constituents of the development process.

Human Resource Development, in the organisational context, is a process by which employees of an organisation are continuously helped in a planned way:

- To acquire capabilities (knowledge, perspectives, attitudes and values and skills required to performed various tasks or functions associated with their present or future expected roles.
- To develop their general enabling capabilities as individuals so that they are able to discover and utilise their own inner potential for their own or organisational development purposes; and
- To develop an organisational culture where superior subordinate relationships team work and collaboration among different subunits are strong and contribute to the organisational health, dynamism and pride of employees.

However, in the National context, Human Resource Development is a process by which the people in various groups (age groups, regional groups, socio-economic groups, community groups, etc). are hatred to acquire new competencies continuously so as to make them more and more self-reliant and simultaneously develop a sense of pride in their country. Such self-reliance and sense of pride could be developed through a variety of interventions at National, Regional and Organisational levels.

Human Resource Development could be initiated and facilitated by the HRD departments, but achievement of its goals depends entirely on various implementing agencies. At the organisational level, these are the line managers and at the National level, these are the various agencies and agents working for development. Some organisations in India have taken a lead in defining and implementing HRD in its perspective.

Basically HRD involves two issues; relationship of the person to (i) on self and (ii) to the society. A person may be an asset or a liability to himself and the society depending upon the development of his skills and abilities and his social attitudes and values. As depicted in the figure below a person relates himself to his own self and to the society through his self-image, social attitudes and values and his work.

Figure 1.1: Relationship of the Person,with Self and Society.

Person	Self Society

Self - Image	:	W
Ideals	:	O
Attitudes	:	R
Values	:	K

The first step in the development of HRD is of course, the development of the abilities and the work competence of the person, HRD cannot be considered as only the development of the resources or abilities in the individual, it has to be combined with one's social commitment HRD, therefore, should aim at the development of professional competence as well as professional attitudes. Another way of looking at HRD is to identify the main factors influencing it.

The influence of poverty on health and education is more clear cut and decisive than on self-image and social attitudes. Three main determinants of HRD may be identified, namely health, education and self-image and social attitudes (Table 1.1).

Table 1.1
Determinants of HRD (After Singh 1986)

	Health	
Education Professional Training	Person	Self-Image Social attitudes

Another way of looking at HRD can be to identify the factors in the individuals which determine his personal satisfaction, social utility and work efficacy. These are factors in the personality of the individuals, his attitudes, and professional skill. Broadly speaking, four such factors can be identified namely, (i) Cognitive abilities, e.g., intelligence, (ii) acquired personal traits, e.g., rationality and work commitment, (iii) social attitudes, e.g. altruism, consumerism health population attitudes, and (iv) work competence, e.g. skill and creativity (Table 1.2). Hence, HRD essentially becomes the development of these four factors which are influenced and shaped by SES and socialising agencies of the family, school and mass media.

However, any definition of HRD should cover innate as well as acquired abilities and attitude of the individual and it should also cover the relationship between the self and society. HRD may be defined as the development of abilities and the attitudes of the individuals leading to personal growth and self-actualisation which enables the individuals to contribute to societal well being and development and in achieving personal satisfaction and happiness.

Table 1.2
Development of HRD

	General Potentialities	*Cognitive abilities Intelligence*
Development of Human Resource	Acquired Personal Traits	Rationality Work – Commitment Altruism
	Social Attitude	Consumerism Health population Attitude
	Work Competency	Skill Creativity

Human Resources have both quantitative and qualitative dimensions. Characteristics like the size composition and distribution of population and labour force, the number of hours worked, the output and earnings per head, etc. are quantitatively measurable, and therefore, lend themselves to statistical treatment. The qualitative characteristics like knowledge, skills, aptitudes, values motivations, etc., often lack conceptual and emotional clarity and precision, and do not lend themselves as easily to statistical treatment as the quantitative characteristics. In many cases, there are conceptual and practical difficulties in distinguishing human investments from consumption expenditure. Although the expenditure on education, health and nutrition tend to enhance the individual's mental and physical capacities and hence, like all other physical investments, contribute to the national output and services, they are not conventionally treated as investments nor are they taken into consideration.

Human Resource Development (HRD) thus is a process which starts with the self and extends. Since the possibilities and potentials of development are limitless, the process is also ongoing. As the individual occupies the role of a first line Manager, this process apart from his efforts for self development, reflects in his concern for those working with him in his section/department also.

Human Resource Development is concerned with the development of human resources in an organisation. Development means improving the existing capabilities of the human resources in the organisation and helping them to acquire new capabilities required for the achievement of the corporate as well as individual goals. HRD believes that individuals in an organisation have unlimited potential for growth and development and that their potential can be develop and multiplied through appropriate and systematic efforts. Given the opportunities and by providing the right type of climate in the organisation individuals, can be helped to given full expression of their potentials contributing to the achievement of the goals of the organisation and thereby ensuring optimisation of human resources. Investment in human beings is another underlying concept of the human resources system. The organisation accepts that the development of human resources involves investment of time and converts for growth. HRD efforts are organisation-wide. Everyone in the organisation will have taken self responsibility for growth and optimisation of performance.

However, three factors that form the basis of the concept of Human Resource Development (HRD) are:

- Its emphasis one emotional and psychological approach to the issues that relate to people.
- Its objective for continuous individual growth a view for narrowing down the gap between the individuals and organisational goals through a process of integration, and
- Its commitment to the philosophy of development for the achievement of this integration.

A great degree of emphasis in HRD is laid on processes so that we may take not of the human factors that go into the performance as well as the product. HRD, in other words, is not a quantitative methods but a process approach to the personnel's needs of an organisation.

The concept of human resources development thus aims at a better understanding of people, their needs and hopes. It also seeks to generate awareness among them of their role as a resource to the organisation for attainment of its goals and objectives, thus minimising the areas of conflict between the two and promoting and integrated approach.

The development of human resources is both a means and an end. Education, cultural expression and improved health are desirable in themselves. But they are also an essential base for social and economic development. Recognising this, a special effort has been made in the Seventh Plan to reorient and accelerate the pace of human resource development. In the field of education in particular the New Education Policy 1986 marks the beginning of a new epoch.

A major theme of the Seventh Plan is the integration of human resource development programmes with other programmes. Some progress has been made towards this. First, integration between different activities within the sector has been promoted, e.g. between health care and family welfare. Second, integration between health, education and related sectors has been pursued, e.g. between child care and pre-primary education, between education, health and nutrition in the integrated child health care and enrollment and retention in the School Health Programmes. Third, human resource development activities e.g. by the use of National Rural Employment Guarantee Programme (NREGP) funds for constructing school and health centre building. The objective of integration is also reflected in the formation of a Ministry of Human Resource Development at the Center.

In the Seventh Plan, the thrust areas in the education sector are (i) Universal elementary education; (ii) Eradication of illiteracy in the age group 15-35 years; (iii) Vocationalisation and skill training programmes at different levels of education; (iv) Upgradation of standards and modernisation at all stages of education with effective links with the world of work and development with special emphasis on science and environment and on value orientation; (v) Spread of education of high quality and excellence in every district in the country; and (vi) Removal of obsolescence and modernisation of technical education, especially to meet emerging requirements.

In the Seventh Plan Document it was pointed out that the commencement of the Seventh Plan coincides with a comprehensive review of the education policy. The achievements in the field of education since 1947 have been impressive and the general formulations of the 1968 policy were unexceptionable.

But they did not get translated into a detailed strategy of implementation accompanied by the assignment of specific responsibilities and financial and organisational support. As a result, problems of access, quality, quantity, utility and financial outlays assumed massive proportions necessitating a new formulation. The National Policy of Education was adopted in May, 1986 and its Programmed of Action was adopted in August, 1986.

These call for comprehensive efforts covering a wide rage of concerns and comprising both long term and medium term measures. These emphasise the need for careful planning and prioritisation with a feasible time-frame within which adequate academic, technical, legislate, financial and administrative inputs may be made available in a coordinated manner. Among the areas on which the policy envisages concerted action are (i) early childhood care and education and integrated child development service, (ii) universalisation of elementary education through formal and non-formal methods so as to relaise the goal by 1995, (iii) reduction of wastage and involvement of local community in the management of elementary education, (iv) vocationalisation of education in order to divert 10 per cent of students as plus two stage to the vocational stream by 1990 and 25 per cent 1995, (v) selective support to R and D infrastructure in higher education system including COSIST programme and critical areas of research, (vi) cultural heritage and curriculum, and (vii) media and educational technology.

Some of these objectives are time-bound and target-specific while some others would take time to get fully incorporated into the national education system. In a few case, interdisciplinary investigation may be necessary for exploring the subject areas and for identifying policy initiatives. It is realised that successful implementation of the policy would depend the extent to which the interface between education, human resource development and socio-economic system is strengthened towards a mutually reinforcing endeavour as contemplated in the Seventh Plan. The implementation some major provisions of the National Policy of Education (1986) have been taken on hand in 1987-88 and several new progammes have been initiated by the Central Government.

It may be relevant to point out there that in pursuance of the National Policy on Education, the target dates laid down in the Seventh Plan for realising universal elementary education and for eradication of illiteracy among the population in the age group of 15-35 years have been reassessed and fixed to end with the Eighth Plan, i.e. 1995. In the case of vocationalisation of secondary education, the policy lays down specific milestone for 1990 and 1995, viz. 10 per cent and 25 per cent of the student enrolment at the higher secondary stage to be provided for in national system.

Human Resources Issues as Determinants of Child Labour

While poverty, literacy levels and access to free and compulsory education, urbanisation, cultural attitudes and decline of rural economies are the fundamental causes of child labour, as variables they do not always impact logically in the statistics when comparison between the Indian States are examined.

Of the 13.5 million child labourers estimated by the 1981 Census, 85 per cent were concentrated in the ten states of Andhra Pradesh, Madhya Pradesh, Maharashtra, Uttar Pradesh, Bihar, Karnataka, Tamil Nadu, Rajasthan and Orissa. Andhra Pradesh has the highest number of total child labourers and in terms of per capita. Tamil Nadu has the highest number of urban child labourers. (Gathia, 1995).

However, between 1971 and 1981, the highest growth of child labourers occurred outside these States, with Jammu and Kashmir, (55.7%), Delhi (41.2%) and Meghalaya (30%), taking the lead according to the 1981 Census, (Gathia, 1995). The statistics could be explained that conflict that breaks down social infrastructures and mass migration to major urban centers could dramatically increase the number of child labourers.

The key to understanding these paradoxical statistics may lie in the success of the State of Kerala, who in the same time period recorded a dramatic decrease in child labour, (48.2%). This could be explained by the unique Kerala socialist experiment in social development which emphasised elementary education and social consciousness as a primary State objective, (Gathia, 1995).

This seems to indicate that poverty alone is not the single biggest cause of child labour. Bihar and Uttar Pradesh which has the highest poverty index are not the states with the highest numbers of child labourers. Kerala with a high poverty index of 26.8 per cent has a low child labour participation rate of 1.2 per cent urban and 1.5 per cent rural. Poverty is more likely to result in child labour in states that have a high level of urban poverty, such as Uttar Pradesh, Tamil Nadu, Maharashtra, Madhya Pradesh, West Bengal, Karnataka and Andhra Pradesh. Tamil Nadu provides an interesting insight into which human resources issue is most determinant in an urban setting. Tamil Nadu has a high urban literacy rate, 70.9 per cent, but also has a high child labour participation in the urban areas. In urban areas there is some correlation between high adult unemployment and child labour, evidenced by 1986 statistics on Tamil Nadu, Karnataka, Maharashtra, West Bengal, Uttar Pradesh and Andhra Pradesh, which have the largest number of registered unemployed adults, (Gathia, 1995). In contrast, Kerala which has one of the largest percentages of rural unemployed, stands out as a State with a low incidence of child labour, (Gathia, 1995).

The above confusing statistics may still offer an intuitive conclusion that the primary human resources determinants of child labour and strategies to deal with them could be the following:

1. In urban areas, a high incidence of poverty, adult unemployment and mass migration could account for a higher rate of exploitative child labour. Urban and regional development planning, increasing adult employment or providing for social security nets may provide the only long term solutions for urban child labour. In addition it is obvious that there in more need for effective enforcement of the constitutional right to free and compulsory education and enforcement of legal rules against child labour, including eliminating the abuse of the subcontracting system and corruption of labour inspectors.
2. In rural areas, sustainable rural economies must be developed. The State of Kerala has shown that raising literacy levels and enhancing social consciousness against child labour is extremely effective in reducing child labour even in areas of high unemployment and poverty.

Common to both the rural and urban areas is the cultural attitudes that promote large families and discriminate against the female child. Population control strategies and eliminating discrimination against the girl child is essential to long term reduction of exploitative child labour. Finally in both the rural and urban areas, the structure of the labour market and utilisation of technology requiring low skills promote exploitation of children. Restructuring of the labour market and promotion of technologies which require higher skills enhancing productivity and competitive positions could dramatically affect the rates of exploitative child labour.

It is too obvious to state that the insertion of a social clause against child labour in the WTO would not deal with the underlying causes of child labour in India.

Strategic Areas of Intervention for Canada

Canada and other developed nations should focus on the exploitation of child labour in India and indeed other developing nations as a human resources development problem and within the context of scarce resources develop multifaceted strategies to assist India in tackling the problem. These could include the following:

- Assist governments, national institutions, like the Indian National Human Rights Commission and civil society to campaign for implementation of the constitutional right to free and compulsory elementary education.
- Assist the above mentioned entities to raise social consciousness on the value and rights of children for the good of the future of their communities.
- Assist the above mentioned entities to undertake direct programming in the fields of non-formal education attached to the workplace, health care, legal aid and formal educational facilities in areas of high incidence of child labour.
- Assist the above mentioned entities to investigate, in particular, the exploitation of child labour in hazardous industries and the agricultural sector and disseminate the results among the communities affected to raise social

consciousness, locally, nationally and internationally that community involvement is needed to stop the exploitation. There are some hazardous industries, such as the gem polishing industry which has not been investigated for analysis as to long term solutions to child labour in this industry. This is despite the fact that it is one of the highest foreign exchange earning sectors that exploit child labour.

- Assist the above mentioned entities to fashion appropriate human resources development policies and implementation programs, including regional development, poverty alleviation and social security systems in areas of high concentration of child labour.
- Assist the above mentioned entities to target the abuse and discrimination of the female child, even if it means challenging cultural traditions.
- Assist the above mentioned entities in reduction of environmental degradation in the rural areas and assist in developing alternative sustainable rural economies.
- Assist the above mentioned entities to develop and promote, among industrial sectors that use child labour, technologies which eliminate the need for child labour but also improve productivity and competitive positions.

The Canadian Government and Canadian expertise could also liaise in India and other developing countries with international organisations who are developing expertise in the area of child labour such as the ILO, UNDP and UNICEF. However, fear of unfair international attention may cause some countries like India to permit only bilateral assistance in the field of exploitation of child labour.

Universalisation of Elementary Education

The target indicated in the National Policy on Education is to achieve universal primary education up to the age of 11 by 1990 and education of all children up to 14 years of age by 1995. A major effort in the Seventh Five-Year Plan was to extend formal school educational facilities organise meaningful non-formal education programmes and to improve the quality, relevance, effectiveness and usefulness of elementary education. Special attention was to be paid to the promotion of education of girls, first generation learners and children from Scheduled Castes/Tribes. The extension of elementary education is a part of the minimum needs programme.

While the Seventh Plan enrolment target for classes I-V is likely to be achieved by the end of the first three years of the plan, it is likely to realise only 40 per cent of the enrolment at the middle school stage by then. Special attention is, therefore, called for here, in the remaining period of the Plan, so that necessary programmes and momentum are developed to help realise 100 per cent enrolment by 1995. Also the progress has not been even in all the states. Taking boys and girls together, the progress of enrolment in classes I-V has been slow in Karnataka, Orissa and Rajasthan. In several states, the gross enrolment ratio was above 100 in classes I-V at the beginning of the Seventh Plan. It was then assumed that this stage, with the improvement of educational institutions and introduction of non-detention policy, the wastage rate would be reduced to the minimum, the proportion of overage and under aged children in the elementary education would be reduced gradually and that enrolment would be stabilised and maintained at a ratio or 100. All this has not happened. Thus, effective steps are required to be taken to remove stagnation in the schools.

Eradication of Adult illiteracy

Eradication of illiteracy in the age group 15-35 years has been accorded a high priority in the Seventh Plan and is regarded a major thrust area. It is one of the components of the Minimum Needs Programmed. The Seventh Plan target was to cover all such illiterates (90 million). In the first two years Seventh Plan, about 14.5 million of people were covered. For 1987-88, the target is to over 8.92 million of people. The National Policy on Education has reiterated the emphasis on the eradication of illiteracy. According to the Programmed of Action, 40 million people in the age group of 15-35 will be covered in the Seventh Plan and the remaining 60 million in the Eighth Plan. Various evaluation studies have brought out that the existing programme of Rural Functional Literacy Project (RFLP) which influences the State Adult Educational Programme (SAEP) and the programme of assistance to Voluntary Agencies (VA) suffers from several inadequacies relating to motivation, training of functionaries, teaching materials, physical facilities, supervision and post-literacy and continuing education activities. The work of voluntary agencies has also recently been evaluated by Joint Evaluation Teams (JETs) previous experience has also underlined the fact that programme of literacy can become meaningful only when they along with the package comprising practical information and skills relevant to day to day needs of learners. All these deficiencies are sought to be made good in the National Literacy Mission.

The objectives of the Mission include identification of areas in which science and techno pedagogic inputs are essential and feasible, identification of institutions which can contribute in technology and pedagogic research and support creation of nation-wide network of training of field functionaries, creation of environment conducive to teaching learning process of adults, reorganisation and harnessing of all ongoing programmes of adult education and literacy as well as the creation of managerial system for planning, implementation, monitoring and evaluation of the Mission. The programme of mass education through students and other educated people which was launched in 1986, and the ongoing programme of RFLP's/SAEP's/VA's would be strengthened and incorporated in the Mission. Along with the programme of eradication of illiteracy programme for imparting functional knowledge and skills and also awareness about the socio-economic development would undertake. Special attention is being given to post- literacy follow up and continuing education through a network of Janashikshan Nilayames. It has been suggest that a National Authority for Adult Education (NAAE) be set up to implementation, monitoring and evaluation of the several programmes at the national level.

Problem of Child Labour and Human Resource Development

Children are an end and means of progress and, therefore, they are wealth and future of a nation. Hence, it is the responsibility of the society to undertake every measure which may be instrumental in the fullest development of children on whom our future depends. Childhood is the stage which shapes the future of an individual and at this stage child requires opportunities for its physical, mental and personality development through all childhood activities and experiences. Younger children also help the adult members of family in household work. Children belonging to agriculturist families participate in some light agricultural activities and children of artisans and craftsmen get training in the family crafts at an early age. But it is also a reality of today that children are working for wages and sometimes under such conditions where the opportunities of proper personality development are denied. When the work undertaken by children affects their health, deprives from education, denies opportunities to play recreation, minimises the chances of intellectual development, it is of paramount importance to protect and promote their interests.

Association of children with work existed in different forms in every society through the history. The committee on child labour (Government of India) pointed out, "Child Labour is not 11 new phenomenons to our age. It has existed in one form or another in all historical times". In India, in earlier times children were given apprenticeship training in the family based occupations like agriculture, crafts and trades to prepare them to take up responsibilities latter on. They learnt the skills by participating in such activities. The work was instrumental in their personality growth.

In the medieval period, a class of landless labourers came into existence and for its survival this class was bound to work for the landowners. Children of these landless labourers helped their parents in the household work and also started to take part in gainful activities outside the house. After the advent of factories, children started to be employed on forms as well as in the factories being cheap and uncomplaining in comparison to adults.

At present a large number of children are engaged in almost all sectors of the economy and performing a variety of jobs. The jobs performed by children and the conditions in which they work; has converted their work into child labour. When participation of children in economic activities conflicts with the physical, mental or personality growth of children, it becomes exploitation. The committee on child labour has pointed out, "Labour becomes an absolute evil in the case of the child when he is required to work beyond his physical capacity, when hours of employment interfere with his education, recreation and rest, when his wages are not commensurate with the quant of work done when the occupation he is engaged are dangerous to health and safety".

Children's Work Construction on Human Resource Development

Child labour has negative effects on Human Resource Development. Children are likely to severe their health conditions by undertaking employment at an early age. As working children come from poor families and they suffer from malnutrition, their work raises their nutritional requirements, which they are mostly unable to meet. Children come into close contact, in work situations, with infective cases of tuberculosis and other communicable diseases, sometimes children do the dirty jobs like rag picking, etc.

The health of children engaged in some occupations adversely affected by poisoning from welding, businesses, textile manufacturing, etc. The health of children working in factories also affected by air pollution, sound of the machines, contact with chemicals, gases, industrial rubbish, etc. sometimes children work more than their capacity or for long hours which affects their health labour has also an adverse psychological impact on children. The physical and emotional stress of work, lack of opportunities to play physical and emotional abuse and neglect, separation from family an apprehension of dark future and the burden of responsibility etc. are some factors which adversely affect the personality development.

(a) Legislation

Child is the most important asset of any nation. It is the responsibility of the state to provide protection to children. Pandit Jawaharlal Nehru once remarked that "the children must be given first place in our thought". As the labour is injurious to physical, mental, moral and social development of children, some special measures are required to protect them from various kinds of the negative effects of the work undertaken by them. There are an appreciable number of legislative enactments which exclusively deal with or have provisions relating to minimum age of employment, hours of work, prohibition of children's employment in certain occupation minimum wages, health and other conditions of work, etc.

The first step in this regard was taken in 1881 when Indian Factories Act, 1881 was passed which provided protection to children employed in factories by fixing minimum age of employment and hours of work. A number of legislative enactments followed with a view to protect and promote the interests of child workers. The Constitution of India has prohibited the employment of children below the age of 14 years in factories, mines or any hazardous employments. It has been laid down under the Directive Principles of State Policy that the State shall direct its policy towards securing that health and strength of workers, men and women and the tender age of children are not abused, and that citizens are not forced by economic necessity to enter vocations unsuited to their age or strength. Childhood and youth are to be protected against exploitation. The Constitution not only prohibited the employment of children up to age of fourteen years but also provided for free and compulsory education of children, guaranteed them protection against exploitation, moral and material amendment. A number of laws having a banning on employment of children have been passed after adoption of the Constitution not only by Parliament but various state legislatures also. The latest enactment in this regard is Child Labour (Prohibition and Regulation) Act, 1986 with a aim to prohibit the engagement of children in certain employments and regulate the conditions of work of children in certain other employments. India is among signatories to various ILO conventions.

(b) A Social-Economic Problem

Child Labour is a socio-economic problem and not a matter which can be solved by mere legislation. Most of the acts enacted where only applicable to the workers in organised sector whereas, the majority of children work is unorganised sector. The committee on Child Labour observed that "the problem of child labour, by and large, has lost its poignancy in the orgnised sector of employment but has assumed alarming proportions in the unorganised sector".

The main reason of the child labour in India is the widespread poverty. Poverty compels millions of children to sell their labour at an age at which they should have gone to school. Children accept work even in unjust conditions when the income of their family is not sufficient to meet the basic requirements of the family. Poverty is the cause as well as consequence of the child labour. According to Mendelivich, a vicious circle exists between poverty and child labour. "There is in fact a vicious circle here: on the one hand, child labour increases unemployment among adults and reduces their incomes, on the other, the unemployment and low wages of adults force them to put their children to work in order to boost the family income. Thus, child labour simultaneously increases and reduces the family income, but as is clear, it reduces rather than increase that income."

(c) Remarks

Child labour is a socio-economic problem. There is an immediate need to improve the working and living prospects of working children. The National Commission on Labour has also recommended that. "The employment of children is indeed more of as economic problem than anything else. Nevertheless, we consider denial of opportunity to children for their proper physical development and education to be issue of a serious nature. Keeping in view the larger interests of the society, while the given the child the necessary education in his more respective years we feel this can be ensured by fixing the employment of hours of children so as to enable them to attend to schooling. When the number of children is adequate, the employers, with the assistance of State Government should make arrangements to combine work with education."

At the total abolition of child labour is not possible in short-term, at least employments of children in hazardous occupations requires removal immediately. Existing laws should be enforced strictly to remove children from hazardous occupations where children's employment is not prohibited, health, education, work load, hours of work, wages and other conditions which are essential for proper physical and mental development of children should be improved. The Committee on Child Labour has also recommended that "As long as poverty continues to exist in its present form, it will be difficult to totally eliminate child !abour. Any attempt to abolish it through legal course will obviously be not a practical provision. In these circumstances the only alternative left will be to ban child labour in hazardous work in other areas, so that child labour ceases to be antithetical to growth and development."

Chapter - 2

CHILD LABOUR: AN OVERVIEW

Meaning of Child Labour

The term 'Child Labour' means different things to different societies. A universally accepted definition of child labour is not available. There is difference between Child Labour and Child Work. 'Child Work' refers to occasional light work done by children which in most of the societies is considered to be an integral part of the child's socialisation process. While helping parents at home and in family farms, children learn to take responsibility and pride in their own activities, activities, acquire certain skills and prepare themselves for the tasks of adulthood. 'Child Labour' implies something different in which young people are being exploited, or overworked or deprived of their rights to health, their overall physical, mental and social growth.

The distinction between both child work and child labour may be briefly stated as follows:

Child Work	*Child Labour*
• Light work (Children learn to take responsibilities)	• Hard and hazardous work, exploitation
• Respect of children's right to health and education	• Deprivation of rights to health and education
• Occasional	• Constant & for long hours
• Legal	• Illegal

Definitions of Child Labour

Child labour is defined, as per the Encyclopedia of Social Science, as "When the business of wages earning or of participation in self or family support conflicts directly or indirectly with the business of growth and education, the result is child labour".

According to ILO, "Child Labour includes children prematurely leading adult lives, working long hours for low wages under conditions damaging to their health and to their physical and mental development, sometimes separated from their families, frequently deprived of meaningful educational and training opportunities that could open up for them a better future."

The Operations Research Group based in Vadodara, defines child labour as a "a child falling within the five to fifteen age bracket and who is engaged in remunerative work may be paid or unpaid, and busy in any hour of the day within or outside the family. . ."

All children out of school are child labour. Being out of school is equal to worst form of child labour 'hazardous' intolerable circumstances and 'harmful to the overall growth and development of the child'.
Source: Government of Andhra Pradesh.

Magnitude of the Problem

Problem of child labour is more acute in developing countries. The accurate and precise estimate of the overall magnitude of child labour, either from a qualitative or quantitative point of view, is virtually not possible due to predominance of informal and unorganised nature of the labour market. The problem of estimating the child labour force becomes all the more complicated and complex on account of the multiplicity of concepts, modes of measurement and the source of information for data collection.

According to the recent experimental survey carried out by the ILO's bureau of statistics, there are at least 120 million children between the age of 5-14 years who are fully at work, and more than twice as many of those for whom work is a secondary activity. Of these, 61 per cent are found in Asia, 32 per cent in Africa and 7 per cent in Latin America. According to a 1997 UNICEF Report, of 250 million children suffers in the world, over one-third are in India. ILO's study on the exploitation of young children in hazardous industries in the developing world, states that, as many as 200 million children under the age of 15, are workers, excluding those who help on family farms and small holidays.

As per an estimate made by the Planning Commission, there were about 17.4 million working children in the country during 1981 and the number is expected to increase to over 20 million working children by the year 2000. As per the 1991 Census, there are 11.29 million child labour, of these 6 million are males and 5 million are females (excluding J&K), the state with the highest child population in the country is Andhra Pradesh, having 1.66 million working children. Other states where the child labour population is more than 1 million are M.P., U.P. and Maharashtra. The incidence of child workers in Urban India has improvement between 1971 and 1991 are Kerala, Tamil Nadu and Gujarat. The situation got substantially worse in U.P. and Orissa during the same period. Statistical profile of child labour in India (1961-91) indicates that in 1991, 42.50 per cent of child labours are agricultural labourers, 35.20 per cent cultivators, 9.10 per cent are in manufacturing activities, 10.20 per cent are in other works. Thus, a disproportionately higher percentage of workers are located in rural areas.

It is clear that child labour is increasing at an alarming rate. There is an urgent need of its solution through proper implementation of laws, through social awareness and though proper policy planning. Let us try to find out the causes responsible for the continuation of this evil problem.

Causes and Consequence of Child Labour

The causes of child labour are many and interrelated. Generally, it may be said that children are compelled to work because of their poor socio-economic conditions. Though poverty is said to be the major factor of child labour yet it is not the only factor, children are also structure of the economy, level and peace of development also influence the extent and nature of child labour. As the reasons of child labour are clubbed with many factors, it is not possible to identified the classification, however, an attempt is made to categorize under the following the heads.

(a) Poverty

The most important factor forcing children to taken up employment is poverty. In India, a developing country, where 60 per cent of the population lives below the poverty line, parents are compelled by poverty to send their children to seek employment: children are forced to work with a view to supplementing in the family income.

(b) Family Size

Even though there is a considerable change in the attitude of the families and majority of the people adopt small family norms, there has not been any major change. A family, which consists of six children, is a normal scene in the rural areas. The needs of the family are dependent on the size of the family. When the need goes up, there is bound to be an increase in the expenditure. This leads to the burden of earning more which has to be borne by all the family numbers irrespective of age. Thus, this is when children engaged in work.

(c) Economic Constraints

Assuming that the members a family can earn their livelihood even without engaging children in work, they are taken aback when the question of spending on education arises. Education is not altogether free. One is required to buy books, uniforms and stationery. Added to this, sometimes tuition fee has to be paid. This means that the poor parents have to earn not only for survival but also to meet the expenses of their children's education. As per the assessment of the PROBE survey, a minimum of Rs. 318 is incurred annually towards the education of one child per year.

If a family fails to earn enough, they are bound to discourage their children form studying.

(d) Caste Factor

The economic structure of the society is influenced by the caste factor. Social cultural and traditional factors are equally responsible for the plight of children in India. Traditionally, children of the upper caste families begin their lives in schools according to their culture whereas children of the lower caste start their lives in work according to their family culture. The families in lower strata though they may not be below the poverty line, send their children to earn skills at different work places. Children are taught a traditional craft at an early stage to make them proficient in a job, which would then be a source of income to them. It is recongnised fact that in childhood body is more flexible to acquire posture required for particular job. Examples, Carpet, Weaving, Pottery, Silk and Cotton weaving, Wood carving etc.

(e) Curriculum

This is also a factor which is responsible for 'push outs'. Curriculum should be set taking grater care. Lengthy, monotonous chapters discourage a child. Research in this aspect is necessary. Proper curriculum that will also be useful for their future is required.

(f) Infrastructure

In villages, most of the schools have two or three rooms. It is difficult to run two to three classes simultaneously in one room. Lack of infrastructure also leads to increase in the drop out rate and subsequently to the increase in child labour.

(g) Distance

In rural areas, the schools are in most cases at a greater distance from home. It is not surprising that children walk or cycle 10-20 kilometers a day to attend school. This proves as discouraging factor. Girl students, especially, are prone to dropout as result of distance.

(h) Psychological

The general below par living conditions in rural areas makes the children and their parents prefer employment, rather than education. Lazy and selfish nature of the parents and other adult members of the family is another factor which make in accord priority jobs.

Consequence of Child Labour

In many countries, children join the labour force at a very early age. Labouring at an early age has many adverse consequences for children. Children employed in carpet weaving, match and fife work, glass and bangles, slate/ pencils, diamond cutting and polishing, lock making etc. are continuously exposed to various hazards, including at times, physical, social, sexual, and psychological abuses. Children can be seen working underground, under water, at dangerous heights or in confined spaces, handling dangerous machines, equipment, tools and sometimes, heavy loads. There is continuous exposure to hazardous substances or extreme temperature or noise levels. They also work for long hours or during the night. Through child labour, the child's potentials are put in improper use for the employers' benefits (Singh and Sekar 2003).

(a) Health Hazards

The adverse consequences of children working in hazardous occupations are many. Firstly, it poses a challenge to the safety of the workers. Secondly, health hazards have more long-term implications in terms of making the person invalid for any work at an early age. Various studies have shown that the impact of the hazardous work begins to show in its severe form only after 2-3 years in terms of morbidity, fever, cold, cough, dysentery, body ache and weakness, tuberculosis and other respiratory problems (Bimal 2000).

The ILO Report of the Director General in the 68th Session of the International Labour Conference, 1983 observed that the vulnerability of working children to health hazards is increased by the high incidence of malnutrition and undernourishment, in contrast to their increased requirement for energy utilization to perform heavy work activities. The incidence of communicable diseases is always higher among these children. Children come into close contact in work situations with infective cases of tuberculosis and other similar diseases. Severe malnutrition, ȧnemia, hard labour, fatigue and inadequate sleep make them more susceptible to infectious diseases.

(b) Psychological Consequences

Many psychologists believer that childhood is the critical period for later development of personality and the exploitative situations of child labour exert strong influence on the child's self-concept and self-esteem. Children growing up in such a negative atmosphere feel mental, social and emotional development. At times, street children and the self-employed children are charged with vague offenses such as vagrancy or loitering. They are often arbitrarily rounded up and detained simply because they are on the streets and appear to be homeless. These children are subjected to physical and emotional abuse. Emotional abuse may take a number of forms such as verbal assault, including threats of sexual or physical abuse, close confinement such as locking a child in a room, and withholding of food (International Encyclopedia of Psychology 1996).

(c) Future Prospects

Deprivation of education and vocational training also has a telling effect on working children. The future of a working child is endangered, as he cannot go to school, or is bound to leave school prematurely, or is unable to coordinate the two activities. He lacks fundamental general and professional knowledge, which is required for normal mental and intellectual development and for making the child into a skilled worker and enabling him to prosper in social and occupational fields. Children thus find themselves locked in unskilled, low paying, unpleasant and unsafe working situations and permanently disadvantaged in the labour market. Ennew is of the opinion that as adults they are not only unemployed but also unemployable (Ennew 1986).

Magnitude of the Problem–World Wide

The number of working children in the world is not yet enumerated precisely by any organisation. Only U.S. Census of Occupations gathers data in a systematic way and even this date is not accurate and there are traces of invisible child labour in some parts of U.S. also. Fuller (1963) confirms that the extent of child labour as a social evil is determinable only by methods of qualitative analysis, with consideration of the character of the actual jobs in which children are engaged, the dangers to which they are subjected in their work and the desirable opportunities to which they are deprived by reason of their being 'gainfully occupied'.

The recent experimental surveys by the ILO's bureau of statistics indicate that an estimated 120 million children between the ages of 5 and 14 work full time in developing counties (UN, 1998). The number increase to 250 million children between the ages of 5 and 14 work full time in developing countries (UN, 1998). The number increases to 250 million if secondary activity is also included (ILO, 1996 b). But out of the estimated 250 million child labour in the world, Asia has the largest number of child workers with 153 million (61%). Where as in Africa and in Latin America, these figures are 80 million (32%) and 17 million (7%) respectively. In relative terms, however, Africa comes first in the proportion of children participating in economic activity, with an estimated 41 per cent of the total number of children aged between 5 and 14 compared to 22 per cent in Asia and 17 per cent in Latin America (ILO, 1999).

Diverse Dimensions of Child Labour

Ever since United Nations declared the year 1979 as the International year of the child, the issue of child labour has been receiving considerable academic reflections and public attention. This, however, does not imply total absences of concern for child labour prior to the UN declaration.

In fact, following the industrial revolution in the Western Europe, there have been piecemeal legal efforts to alleviate the pitiable conditions of child labour. Some efforts are also discernible in the postcolonial countries. Nonetheless comprehensive and systematic cognition of issue at the academic level seems to have been ushered in or at least stimulated by the UN declaration. Perhaps, the accentuation of the miserable conditions of the working children of the world prompted the declaration. That is besides the matter.

In less than a decade, we have excellent descriptive accounts on the living and working conditions of child labour in diverse sectors countries. In addition, there have been persistent attempts to explore the objective conditions operating in the emergence and substantive use of child labour in different socio-political contexts.

Most studies, however, delimit their analysis to the victim's socio-economic background, and thereby reiterate one another. Though these provide a glimpse of the reality, the treatment of phenomenon in isolation from the larger political-economic context and the implicit historicity has considerably reduced academic significance. Of course, documentation of detailed descriptive accounts is a sine gua non for theory building and policy-making. But now that we have considerably progressed in building the documentation, it is time to comprehend the issue totality. There is that an urgent need the develop theoretical perspective to get a better insight into the problem.

The phenomenon of child labour, like all other social phenomena, is historically and socially conditioned. Its emergence growth and nature of dynamics are intrinsically bound with the changing trends in production and reproduction of a given social matrix. By and large, prior to the rise an consolidation of modern capitalism, children were primarily assigned the status of helpers and learner in family occupations-often hereditarily determine in India context under the supervision of the adult family member. In some sense, the workplace was almost an extension of the home and the little workers operated within the genuine framework of personalised and informal milieu. Advent of capitalist relations of production made redundant the traditional practice of family members working as a team. The child worker is thus forced out form the familial environment.

It is a double alienation-separation from the system of production and an expulsion from the family. The job more often than not exposed the child to various kinds of health hazards and the hours of work stretched longer than before.

Nevertheless, the wage earnings remain relatively meager as ever, ill-treatment and unscrupulous exploitation increased unprecedented. The recent studies on child labour hardly provide any significant in sight into the process of historical and social conditioning of child labour.

The serious imperials studies, both in different parts of the country and abroad, though not uniform appear to fall into a patter, in a very broad sense of the term. In order to comprehend the issue a modest attempt is made in the following paras to critically review the existing material on the subject with special reference to the explanations provided for the nature and dynamics of the issue of child labour.

Among the numerous explanations of the rise and growth of child labour. The socio-economic backwardness is considered as one of the most crucial factors. Countries like India with massive and abysmal poverty are said to be fertile grounds for the large-scale employment of children. But as the question of backwardness is relative and cannot be understood in isolation form developed regions, the independence of the factor for analysis is minimal.

Backwardness is a historically specific phenomenon associated with the development of capitalism in the West and its relations of expropriation of the world (Brett, 1973). Colonial and imperial dominations for over four centuries have endangered the survival of the large masses of the Third World Peoples (Arright and Sau, 1973 Fanon, 1966: 119-63).

The consequent unemployment, hunger, poverty and illiteracy forced the children to enter labour force. There are at least two important schools of thought, namely, the dependency and the mode of production, which elicit the reasons for perpetuation of, backwardness and its complex relations with child labour (Johnson, 1983).

The dependency school holds that the extraction and transformation of surplus through a series of metropolis satellite links have been responsible for reproducing conditions of under development in most parts of the world (Frank, 1967). The social contradiction characteristic of capitalism is thus not confined to state societies but to the world system as a whole, wherein the antagonism between the world proletariat is primary (Amin, 1974:30). Historically of course, the technological and financial dependence (Johnson, 1983).

World system approach, however, undermines the internal contradictions with the countries of the underdeveloped world and over-stresses the unity of classes on world scale. True imperialism in a very large is responsible for the destruction of indigenous knowledge, culture, and technology compounded the misery of masses but it could articulate its interests through certain local agencies and institutions. The world system of theory does not answer the question of the motif forces for the dynamics of emancipation form the superimposed backwardness.

On the other, the classical Marxist tradition of analyzing the modes of production of given societies stresses the need to comprehend the dialectical interaction between forces and relation of production. The role of imperial then forms an integral part of this structural analysis. According to this perspective, "the dialectics between forces and relation of production differ in its terms form capitalist relation of production encourages some areas of economy and represses others" (O'Loughlin, 1975:850). In other words, this approach strives to comprehend the entire panorama of colonialism economic expansionism and contradiction with in the underdeveloped societies, Anyway, it hardly needs a reiteration that backwardness of the Third World cannot be understood is isolation form the colonial arid neo-colonial exploitation. We, however, deliberately ignore the classical esoteric psychological theories, cultural relativity, peasant passivity, and other worldliness of the eastern regions as instances of the intrinsic ethnocentrism of the western scholars and propagandists.

In the case of India, prior to the colonial invasion, all the religious upheavals, dynastic wars, and intervention if put together, could not bring about any structural reorganisation of the economic base. The British annexation brought for the first time a profound change in the economic structure, unheard of in the past dozens of centuries.

The introduction of capitalist conception of land and land revenue system, extraction or raw materials for the industries of England, rapid commercialisation of Indian agriculture, the establishment of certain industries, import of manufactured goods, etc., led to increasing disorganisation of the India handicrafts (Desai, 1966:7-30). As a consequence, there was a large masses of the peasantry. The man made famines accelerated the process of creation of the cheap wage labour. In short, exploitation and stagnation were the order of the day. The post-colonial situation did not qualitatively alter the domination of imperialism. It has been conclusively substantiated that the net effect of foreign investment is create an outflow of capital from the perinhery to methropolis (Muller, 1973).

After five decades of independence, India has remained one of the poorest countries of the world (Mendelivitt. 1979: 213). Also, the proportion of child workers to total child population in different regions demonstrates a relatively high percentage in South Asia (5.4), Africa (4.0) and Latin America (2.6), (Kurukshetra, 1978: 4). Incidentally, India possesses the highest child labour force in the world.

Of course, with 248 million children it also accounts for 16 per cent of the total children of the world. According to 1971 census, about 10.7 million children were engaged in labour and constituted around 6 per cent of the Indian labour force (Government of India, 1979:14). Broadly marking a similar correlation between backwardness and intensity of child labour use, the different states in the country reflect a variation of 1 to 12 per cent of the child labour in the total labour force the highest being in Dadra and Nagar Haveli (11.6%) and Arunachal Pradesh (10.5%). Government of territories are backward in comparison to the most parts of the country, there is also little direct penetration of imperial capital. The nature of production relations in these backward regions with indigenous population indicates the significance of sociological factors in comprehencing the phenomenon.

In brief, these simple official data force us to seek the help of world system theory mode of production analysis and the sociology of specific cultures and environment. We shall return to this complex relations in a whole but suffice here to note that backwardness is not the sufficient condition or understanding the phenomena of child labour.

Likewise the issue of poverty, a very relative and subjective concept (Horwitz, 1969: 20), is inadequate-though necessary to satisfy the intellectual urge. True, the association between child labour and the poverty in any space and time would be significant. But it would still remain as a cognition at an empirical, isolated and sectoral level. In fact when between 250 and 300 million people are in condition of near starvation (Raychaudhury, 1985:801-6), not poverty alone but possibly the relations to land and other productive assets may give an idea of the families involved in child labour.

As we are aware that the bottom half of the rural households in India own only 4 per cent of the land, and 27 per cent and 30 per cent are tenants and agricultural labourers respectively (Government of India, 1979: 10-11), and over 30 per cent live below the minimum level of income (Da Costa, 971:54-55), the origin of child labour for these families is little surprising. But this speaks only a little. So also one-third of the urban population in India lives in abject poverty. A study in Madras noticed that 98.8 per cent of the families of the working children have an income of less than Rs. 500 per month (George, 1975). Similar is the position in Delhi and Mumbai with 88 per cent and 78 per cent respectively, earning less than Rs. 500 a month. Abject poverty causes diseases and other forms of disabilities which very often cause imbalance in family budget and force the poor parents to send their children for work.

Bondage is a product of abject poverty. It would be pertinent that almost 73 per cent of the total child labour force in rural areas and urban unorganised sectors are put under diverse forms of bandage by their own parents or guardians (Juval et al., 1985:73. Ganguly, 1984: and Singh et al. 1980). The principal feature is the pledging of child against a loan or an agreement between the employer and parents of child that child will work all the time, if necessary, in exchange of money or food. In fact, in some villages of Medak district in Andhra Pradesh, it has been found that landlords depend entirely on the labour of bonded children (Rural Wing, NLI, 1977: 539-545). Besides the low level of income, any emergency like medical treatment or some other causes forces the parents to let the child to work without realizing the harm of bondage of children to employer (Marla, 1977:424-430). Sometimes the child once bonded remains bonded till he/she is able to buy freedom by giving his/her offspring in bondage. At times children are forced to sell themselves to repay the loans of the parents (Mundle, 1976:653-656). The nature and character of bondage, however, varies depending upon the existing nature of agrarian.

Similarly, in urban unorganised sectors, the nature of bondage in is no way different. Children are very often pledged by their parents and relatives to the employers specifically in match, bidi and textile industries (Daniel, 1976:6-9: Gangrade and Joseph, 1983: Sharama, 1979:345-52). These children are forced to work between 12 and 16 hours a day. Their meager wages are often adjusted against their parents' debts to the employer or the advances (Mehatha, 1983). This reflects not only the nature of informal sector but also the specific character of Indian capitalism, which survives with the cheapest available labour.

Alongside the economic backwardness and poverty, the peculiar restrictive tradition of learning is said to be one of the factors for the growth of child labour. Historically, learning outside home has remained more or less confined to the privileged members of upper castes where children of producing classes have learned the necessary skills form their parents for their respectively hereditary occupations. Formal education had little, relevance for their survival and development. Despite constitutional commitments and piecemeal efforts at universalisation of education, the fact that nearly two-thirds of the people remain illiterate indicates continuity of the country's population are committed in the culture of work form the beginning. There is little choice. A study in the metropolitan city of Bombay found that 41 per cent of children were working as that was their family tradition (NIPC, 1978). Nonetheless, much cannot be imputed to this factor because it in turn, depends on the actual socio-economic position of the households. Moreover, why the traditional attitude prevails among certain social classes and categories of people and not among other essentially begs analysis of the total social formation in its existence and dynamics.

It is also argued that limited number of schools their absence in several interior villages, the clash of school timings and agricultural operations; and the cost of schooling as well its restricted implications, on job opportunities facilitate the children of underprivileged classes to enter into the labour market. This again is a partial explanation for it ignores both the socio-economic spaces occupied by the households of the child workers and articulation of capital into their matrix and the role of state.

An estimated 90 per cent of non-enrolled children belong to their lowest agrarian classes, namely agricultural labour poor and middle peasants (Acharva, 1982:18-21). Further, of the 140 million rural children in the age group of 5 to 14, over 86 million are not enrolled in the school registers. About 62 per cent of the children in the rural areas do not attend the elementary school (OPS, 1985).

They cannot but belong to the classes and below subsistence level families. In a broad sense, the denial of access to format education ensures the reproduction of the unjust social system. Besides the low enrolment, the drop-out rates are equally high. It increases with every higher grade. Here too, the drop-outs mostly belong to marginal families in rural areas. For every 100 admitted to class is not more 40 go up to class V and less than 25 up to class VIII (Chakravarty, 1972). Dropout rates are higher in backward states and the highest among the scheduled communities and women. In short, the phenomena of child labour and illiteracy manifest and caste and class divisions in the Indian society, land convey the health of Indian Political economy.

In the establishment circles, demographic expansion has been considered as the primary source of child labour. The validity of this explanation, if has been drummed precisely because in the expansion of population its held that the individual citizens are alone responsible. Both the premises are exaggerations and mostly erroneous. Human reproduction is not independent of a given system, and the rationality of individual choice can hardly be questioned.

Needless to stress that it is more to evade a critical issue, in whose genesis and growth the state tangible role than to analyse and resolve the social issue. The major factor influencing fertility rate is the poor socio-economic condition of family (Espendhade, 1972).

How else one can explain high rates of biological reproduction in the backward? Third World countries and among the impoverished small peasants, and insecure wage earners (Mamdani, 1972). Without going to the details, all the available explanations such as backwardness, poverty, cultural inertia, illiteracy, population expansion, etc., offer explanation to only one or the other dimension of the child labour. What is missing is comprehensive holistic and historical analysis of phenomenon? This can only be grasped by placing phenomenon in the total political economy and culture of the country.

Meanwhile, it is worth noting that not only the population below the poverty line has been increasing a faster rate since independence but also unemployment is showing an unprecedented rate of growth. Leaving alone the disguised unemployment and underemployment, the registered unemployed have increase from 2 million in 1966 to 24 million today. Of those who are employed (268 million), only 9 per cent are working in the organised sector (Pathey, 1985). The capacity of organised sector to absorb labour has, in fact, been steadily declining. On the other hand, the informal unorganised sector in relatively expanding and that too in advanced regions. A significant part of the labour in this in secure in formal market is either contractual or bonded, and most of workers belong to the backward regions and lower castes and classes. Not only the backwardness but also progressive mechanization of agriculture has squeezed out a large number of farmlands and forced migration to cities, and of contributed to the acceleration of the growth of child labour (Khandekar, 1970). Most of the 16.5 million child workers accounting for one-third of the total child work force sell their labour power in this petty commodity production. Surely the survival of this dependent and retarded capital roots primarily on the unemployment of large masses of people, built-in disunity in the recruitment of labour and open flouting of labour laws. The children are preferred to certain types of labour where with less than half the adult wage, nearly the same quantum of adult work can be extracted from the child. In almost all the cases, child workers are underpaid and work more hours than usual, with lack of proper facilities in their working areas. Different empirical studies like match factories at Sivakasi, slate and pencil industries in Tamil Nadu, glass bangle industries at Firozabad, carpet weaving in Kashmir and Varanasi, etc., reveal the same facts. The hazards of the work result in chronic bronchitis, anemia, etc. (Punekar, 1975:25-27). Children in rural areas, particularly in mechanised farms, are no way free from such hazards but there is little documentation on the subject many incidents goes unheeded. However, health problems of urban working children are more obvious. In addition, the children also perform several household chores which are unpaid and unrecognised. Unfortunately, the scope of this work does not cover this issue.

In sum, the existing literature on child labour in India is extremely limited. The various committee reports and micro level surveys only indicate certain dimensions of symbolic phenomenal set up and have not gone beyond the appearance of the phenomenon. Invariably, backwardness and poverty are primarily considered as the driving forces, for the employment of children. It in no wonder that the legislative measures have remained more or less-effective, except perhaps in organised industries.

It must, however, be admitted that the most of the literature include either ad hoc at best local descriptions. The precious few important surveys and sociological researches are inadequate to arrive at any generalised proposition on the formation of child labour force. It is, therefore, important to look at issue form a broader perspective which may help us to understand the issue a better. In order to pursue this venture, it is essential to have certain amount to conceptual clarification and operational definitions at the very beginning.

How to Identify a Child Worker

Children were treated as the property of their father and legitimized the institutional violence. This appears as a fertile field of research but as yet little has been done. It is, however, evident that every society has its own notion of childhood, depending on the socio-economic conditions circumscribed by culture, ideology and above all the production relations. With the advent of colonialism, exploitation of children got accentuated. The employers were always at their best to exploit the children by giving a false demarcation of age group to the working children. For instance, the factories Act, 1881, the first ever legislation, defined the child as a person below the age of 17 years. Even the today, there is a lot of divergence in different legislations on the age of child workers. Of the ten major legis1ations in India which include relations to employment of children, five have defined the child as below 15 years of age, three provide for the age 14 one puts between 12 and 14 years and another 12 (Ghatek, 1984:152-53).

The Concept of Labour

The children doing the domestic charge as well working in family production units receive no age. Simultaneously, children are taken as apprentices without any meaningful training and with little or no wage payment, other than perhaps meals and accommodation. Both the forms of abuse of child labour are common in today's developing world. Notwithstanding the innumerable controversies regarding the several dimensions of labour, there seems to be certain broad agreements among the concerned. The notion of labour varies from one production process to the other. In other words, it is conditioned by time and production system contemporarily, the conception of labour in terms of both use and exchange value is well-established and its constitution of exploitation has become a matter of concern. In the light of this, a humble effort is made in the following paras to examine the role of children in different system of production and reproduction.

Child Labour in Different Production Processes

Incidentally, a large per centage of child work force is indirectly but actively involved in concealed production activities under the domination of colonial and imperial forces. The indirectness appears in the form of assistance of parents in the process of selling labour. Unfortunately, this has not yet received the appropriated attention in richly deserves. Be that alone, the role of children in the capitalist labour market is unique form all other types of production processes in the sense that their labour power is bought by capitalist with the sole objective of maximisation of profit. Simultaneously, the capitalist market excludes from consideration massive quantum of work performed by the children in the domestic field, inclusive of family farm and self account-work. Simple use values continue to be produced within the home *via* child labour. But this was never so problematic in the past. The capitalist economy is based on individual ownership of private properly but ironically most people own little or no important private property. The employer is free from the traditional obligation of the feudal lord serf, master-slave relationship and can dismiss the employees whenever their labour is no longer needed. By designating child as miniature adult and engaging them in certain specific works, capitalism justified the discrimination of work of women children and adults and consequently provides basis for dividing the working class in the ultimate interest of capitalism. The domestic unpaid labour permits employers to draw upon the unpaid labour of children to make adult employees more efficient and ultimately facilitates high reproduction labour for capitalists. The marginalisation of child workers has also become conspicuous by making systematic differentiation of from the labour adults as manifest in lower remuneration, and often paid often to their parents, and designation of so-called 'trainees', 'apprentices', 'casual', or temporary of contract laborers' etc. (Aries, 1979). In other words, a large number of children employed by capitalist enterprises are not free to dispose of their labour.

In this context, it may be interesting to not the relevance of the differentiation of child from the adults in labour according to neo-classical and Marxist economics. For the former the differentiation in wages is based on the demand, marginal productivity of labour and supply. The lower wages of children is then explained in terms of demand and supply function of their labour as compared to those of the adults. The lower marginal productivity of children's labour is explained in terms of their being endowed with immature labour, i.e. less skilled than the adults. The cause thus seems to lie outside the economic system, either in the biology or psychology, the latter being based on the structure of preferences.

In contrast, the Marxist approach though admits natural weaker position of children than the adults by virtue of their biological constitution and psychological immaturity, concentrates on the question of how and why children enter into the labour market. Parents send their children to work in capitalist enterprises not because of taste or grater family income or education of the children but because they are objectively pushed into it by the development of the capitalist system. It is the need for expropriation of more and more surplus an insatiable urge of the capitalists-that there is system of gradation of wage and work in addition, the patriarch within the family needs to be conceptual which facilities the process of capital accumulation and reproduces the conditions for its continuity.

Declaration of the Rights of the Child

UN Declaration of the Rights of the Child, 1959: The adoption of the Declaration of the Rights of the Child by the General Assembly of the UN on November 20th, 1959 was indeed a very important event as regards the international recognition of the rights of the child. The General Assembly affirmed that the child has the right to enjoy special protection and to be given opportunities and facilities to be able to develop in healthy and normal manner.

The Declaration had limited interpretation of the rights of the child. The Declaration says that measures should be taken against the social evil of Slavery, Child Labour, Traffic and Prostitution of Minors.

On 20th November 1959, the United Nations unanimously adopted a Resolution on the Rights of the Child. In the Resolutions, the United Nations General Assembly reaffirmed its faith in fundamental human right and in the dignity and worth of the human person. The United Nations proclaimed that everyone is entitled to all the rights and freedoms without distinction of any kind such as race, colour, sex, language, religion, political or other status. The UN Resolution says that the child, by reason of his physical and mental immaturity, needs special safeguards and care, including appropriate legal protection, before as well as after birth.

The Resolution cells upon parents, voluntary organisations, local authorities and national governments to recognise the rights of the child and strive for their observance by legislative and other measures progressively taken in accordance with the following principles:

Principle 1

Every child, without any exception, shall enjoy all the rights.

Principle 2

The child shall enjoy special protection, and shall be given opportunities and facilities, by law and by other means, to enable him to develop physically, mentally, morally, spiritually and socially in a healthy and normal manner and in conditions of freedom and dignity.

Principle 3

The child shall be entitled form his birth to a name and a nationality.

Principle 4

The child shall enjoy the benefits of social security. Special care and protection shall be provided him and to his mother; including adequate pre-natal and post-natal, care.

Principle 5

The child who is physically, mentally or socially handicapped shall be given the special treatment, education and care required by his particular condition.

Principle 6

The child needs love and understanding. He shall, wherever possible, grow up in the care and under the responsibility of his parents and, in any case, in an atmosphere of affection and of moral and material security.

A child of tender age shall not, except in exceptional circumstances, separated from his mother.

Society and the public authorities shall have the duty to extend particular care to those without adequate means of support.

Principle 7

The child is entitled to receive education, which shall be free and compulsory, at least in the elementary stages. He shall be given an education on a basis of equal opportunity, to develop his abilities, his individual judgment and his sense of moral and social responsibility to become a useful member of society.

Principle 8

The child shall in all circumstances be among the first to receive protection and relief.

Principle 9

The child shall not be protected against all forms of neglect, cruelty and exploitation. He shall not be the subject of traffic, in any form.

The child shall not be admitted to employment before an appropriate minimum age.

He shall in no case becaused or permitted to engage III any occupation or employment, which would prejudice his health or education or interfere with his physical, mental or morel development.

Principle 10

The child shall be protected from practices which many foster racial, religious and any other form of discrimination. He shall be brought up in a spirit of understanding, tolerance, friendship among people, peace and universal brotherhood, and in full consciousness that his energy and talents should be devoted to the service of his fellow men.

Impact

The 1959 UN Declaration had a limited effect on the Rights of the Child in the developed as well as developing countries since the Declaration was just a statement of intent or purpose and it did not have any legal binding.

Exactly after 20 years from the 1959 UN Declaration, the United Nations declared the year 1979 as the International Year of the Child.

In response to the UN Declaration of the International Year of the Child, the governing Body of the ILO at its 209th Session held in February-March 1979 endorsed the Declaration and appealed to its member states to apply its standards on the minimum age for admission to employment and the conditions of employment of children.

Further, the ILO appealed to the Member States to take necessary legal and administrative action on the three principles: (1) A child is not a 'small adult' but a person entitled to self fulfillment through work at an early age, (2) Governments should, in cooperation with all the national organisations concerned, take all necessary social and legislative action for the progressive elimination of child labour; and (3) Pending the elimination of Child Labour, it must be regulated and humanized.

Human Rights and Child Labour

The International Labour Organisation (ILO) has estimated that 250 million children between the ages of five and fourteen work in developing countries–at least 120 million on a full time basis. Sixty-one per cent of these are in Asia, 32 per cent in Africa, and 7 per cent in Latin America. Most working children in rural areas are found in agriculture; many children work as domestics; urban children work in trade and services, with fewer in manufacturing and construction.

Child labour ranges from four-year-olds tied to rug looms to keep them from running away, to seventeen-year-olds helping out on the family farm. In some cases, a child's work can be helpful to him or her and to the family; working and earning can be a positive experience in a child's growing up. This depends largely on the age of the child, the conditions in which the child works, and whether work prevents the child from going to school.

The Children's Rights Division at Human Rights Watch has focused its efforts on the worst forms of child labour. Children, who work long hours, often in dangerous and unhealthy conditions, are exposed to lasting physical and psychological harm. Working at rug looms, for example, has left children disabled with eye damage, lung disease, stunted growth, and a susceptibility to arthritis as they grow older. Children making silk thread in India dip their hands into boiling water that burns and blisters them, breath smoke and fumes from machinery, handle dead worms that cause infections, and guide twisting threads that cut their fingers. Children harvesting sugar cane in El Salvador use machetes to cut cane for up to nine hours a day in the hot sun; injuries to their hands and legs are common and medical care is often not available. Denied an education and a normal childhood, some children are confined and beaten, reduced to slavery. Some are denied freedom of movement–the right to leave the workplace and go home to their families.

Some are abducted and forced to work. The human rights abuses in these practices are clear and acute. We have found similar problems in Asia, the Middle East, Latin America, and the United States, children who work for too many hours and too many days, for too little, or sometimes no pay, subject often to physical abuse, exposed to dangerous pesticides, and made to work with too dangerous tools. Our objectives in tackling these aspects of the complex and troubling child troubling child labor issue include drawing attention to the plight of child workers, helping to end these appalling practices, and contributing to the debate on the rights dimension of the larger issue of children and work.

Bonded Child Labour

Bonded labour takes place when a family receives an advance payment (sometimes as little as US $15) to hand a child-boy or girl-over to an employer. In most cases the child cannot work off the debt, nor can the family raise enough money to buy the child back. The workplace is often structured so that 'expenses' and/or 'interest' are deducted from a child's earnings in such amounts that it is almost impossible for a child to repay the debt. In some cases, the labour is generational, that is, a child's grandfather or great-grandfather was promised to an employer many years earlier, with the understanding that each generation would provide the employer with a new worker-often with no pay at all.

Bonded labour is outlawed by the 1956 UN Supplementary Convention on the Abolition of Slavery, the Slave Trade, and Institutions and Practices Similar to Slavery. See also International Legal Standards on Forced and Bonded Labour.

Millions of children work as bonded child labourers in countries around the world; the full extent of the problem has yet to be shown. Millions work in India alone, as documented in the Human Rights Watch 2003 report, Small Change: Bonded Child Labour in India's Silk Industry, and 1996 report, The Small Hands of Slavery: Bonded Child Labour in India. Many bonded children are subjected to severe physical abuse, as in a case cited in the July 1995 Human Rights Watch report, Contemporary Forms of Slavery in Pakistan:

Two years ago at the age of seven, Anwar started weaving carpets in a village in Pakistan's province of Sindh. He was given some food, little free time, and no medical assistance. He was told repeatedly that he could not stop working until he earned enough money to pay an alleged family debt. He was never told who in his family had borrowed money or how much he had borrowed. Any time he made an error with his work, he was fined and the debt increased. Once when his work was considered to be too slow, he was beaten with a stick. Once after a particularly painful beating, he tried to run away, only to be apprehended by the local police who forcibly returned him to the carpet looms.

On the advocacy front, we have met with children's and human rights groups, as well as representatives from the United Nations Children's Fund (UNICEF), the International Labour Organisation (ILO), the World Bank, and other organisations, to try to develop a holistic strategy to prevent children from losing their childhood, education, and opportunities by being entrapped in bonded labour. We have also worked to provide to children's organisations and international advocacy groups objective on-the-spot reporting to support efforts to effect change.

Chapter - 3

CHILD LABOUR: THE GLOBAL SITUATION

Child Labour in Developed and Developing Countries with Special reference to Third World Countries

Laws exist in all continents of the world to prevent the exploitation of the child. Various seminars are being held, resolutions passed and plans of action drawn up on the protection of children, yet not much could have been done about child protection and the problem grows out of proportion day by day. A recent study published by the ILO mentioned that hundreds of millions of children around the world are being forced to work often at dangerous or illegal jobs. And raising number or them have become prostitutes of drug-runners. Many children are employed illegally in dangerous conditions that maim or kill them, while others grow up without education and are condemned to life-long poverty.

Some 200 million children in the Third World are forced to make their own living, many of them under slave-like conditions. From the low-wage labour of these children, some of them as young as five-factory owners profit, but so do consumers in the wealthy nations. Efforts to end this exploitation have been blocked by governments, or by the fear that whole families might starve if the children were not allowed to work. The problem is expected to get worse before it gets better.

Eighty per cent of all Pakistani carpets are made by children under age 15. Few of them make the legally required minimum wage; many are sickened by the wool dust. Children in India, Nepal and Afghanistan too make rugs in order to survive. Children pick tobacco in Indonesia, tea in Sri Lanka, oranges in Brazil.

The cut cocoa beans without ever knowing the tasted of chocolate; they make T-shirts in Bangladesh, handbags in Thailand, and work with dangerous chemicals in Moroccan tanneries. They pan for gold in Peruvian rainforests, cut diamonds in the Indian slums and comb throughout Egypt's jasmine fields starting before sunrise.

Large landowners and companies on the Indian subcontinent employ some 25 million-child slaves, the London human rights organisation Anti-Slavery International (ASI) estimates. Eight million are forced to do slave labour in the Andes, hundreds of thousands are working off their parent's debts on Brazilian plantations and thousands of others are servants in South Africa households.

Child Labour in the third world is something, "We just have to accept", says the advertising director of a German leather-importing company. Since Italian tanneries became too expensive, the German firm has had skins tanned in eastern Pakistan.

Two hundred million children under the age 15 have to earn their own livelihoods, the International Labour Organisation (ILO) says in its annual report. But the number could be three to four times higher according to an ILO expert.

The ILO report says that some as young as 5 and as many as 25 per cent of all children between the ages of 10 and 14 are estimated to be working. Although it is difficult to pinpoint exactly how many are working, since so many are working illegally, the numbers have swelled especially in the developing world. Children have been dragged into prostitution and the drug trafficking in unprecedented numbers and the problem has now reached explosive proportions, says the report. Asia has the largest child work force. In some countries, young people make up to 11 per cent of the labour force. Italy and Spain to the list in Western Europe. In the United States, a government study shows a 250 per cent increase in violations of the child labour laws between 1983 and 1990. While more and more children are put to work as rug weavers, farm labourers, domestic servants, drug runners and prostitutes, only a few nations have taken any meaning full steps to contain the problem.

In the context of global incidence of child labour, a recent report of the US Labour Department has pointed that more than 50 per cent of the world's estimated 100 million to 200 million child labourers are in Asia, and constitute a large part of the work force in parts of Latin America and Africa. The places in Asia rage from the crowded garment factories, where the doors are locked and the children work for 14 hours a day, to small dusty earthen huts which can seat four children to a loom knotting carpet in a pit for hours on end. The above findings have been compiled in a survey of 19 countries, titled as 'Sweat and Toil of Children.' Among the countries surveyed for child employment were: Bangladesh, China, India, Indonesia, Nepal, Pakistan, the Philippines, Thailand, Egypt, Brazil and Colombia. The report shows that in most cases child workers toil for long hours for substandard wages under unhealthy conditions. The Indian Government acknowledges at least 17.5 million working children, the report adds. The country-wise estimates of child labour as provided by the report are as under:

India : 17.5 million according to official reports.

Bangladesh : According to official estimate in 1990, 5.7 million children aged between 10 and 14 were working. Non-governmental estimate put the number at 15 million.

China : Figures not available.

Indonesia : 1990 population census reported 2.2 million children between ages 10 and 14 were working, but this figure does not include child workers below 10 years of age and children involved in domestic work.

Nepal : An estimated 3 million children working in agricultural sector and export oriented carpet industry of the country.

Pakistan : Estimates between 2 million and 19 million child labourers in the agricultural, weaving and goods factory sectors.

Philippines : According to estimates by the Philippines Department of Labour and Employment, the United Nations Education Fund and International Labour Organisation (ILO), between 2.1 million and 5.7 million children are working.

Thailand : Estimates vary greatly but the United Nations put the number at about 4 million children.

Africa : The ILO estimates that one child in three has to work, making up 17 per cent of the content's work force.

Egypt : 4 million children between the ages of 6 and 14 work.

Elsewhere on the continent, children under the age of 14 work in garment factories in Lesotho, on Sisal plantations in Tanzania and Mines for gold and diamonds in Ivory Coast and mine for Chrome in Zimbabwe. In Latin America, the ILO estimates that between 25 per cent and 20 per cent of children work.

Child Labour in the manufacturing and mining sectors can generally be found in home-based garment, small scale mining in remote areas, and to lesser extent, in the assembling plants of Mexico and Guatemala. The number of working children in Latin America is growing according to some experts.

The developing countries have an unemployment rate ranging between 20 and 30 per cent. 100 to 200 million child labourers represent 4 to 8 per cent of the world employment potential of 2.4 million. Replacement of child labourers by unemployed adults could have a major impact on employment prospect in many developing countries.

Abolition of Child Labour-ILO Policy and its Implications

A new Rs.850 crore scheme to eliminate child labour in hazardous industries over a period of 5 years was launched.

(a) The Central Government

The ILO's View: The problem with child labour is that it can be hardly be legislated away, for its roots lie in abject poverty; where social and economic conditions have improved, children go to school and child labour has virtually disappeared. So any society, which wants its children to be free to learn and play, must first free its entire population from fear of want. This means ensuring basic human needs of all people. They include such essentials as food, shelter, clothing, water, education, training and provision of gainful employment.

Mr. Francis Blandchard, the then Director General of the summarised the goals for action in the arena of child labour: "In the long run, the progressive elimination of child labour requires a general improvement of living standards, a reinforcement of the educational infrastructure and perhaps most basically, greater consciousness of the need for change. In the short run, the protection of working children requires practical measures that can improve their working and living conditions."

(b) The Policy and its Implications

Given the intimate link between the child labour and the employment and income status of the households, the provision of schemes that generate and enhance employment and income among adult workers is a necessary condition for the reduction of child labour.

An equally important measure is the promotion of schooling. The need to expand educational facilities and improve the quality of curricula and teaching methods are all too obvious. Feeding programmers could increase enrolment and attendance among school-age children. They could improve the nutritional status of children at school, as well as their cognitive and academic performance. Moreover, it is observed that the larger the income the greater the implicit income transfer to poor households and hence, the greater the like hood that parents will send their children to school rather than to work. Labour legislation must be accompanied by a wide range of measures encompassing employment and income generation and reforms and expansion in education, if the problem of child labour is to be fully dealt with.

Comprehensive attempts made towards elimination of child labour included: (1) dealing with the legal hurdles which impeded practical action by Government The Child Labour (Prohibition & Regulation) Act, 1986 set in a legal context the priority areas for Government action and provide legitimacy for the Government in the design and implementation of programmes for working children; and (2) formulation of a national policy on child labour intended to deal with the socio-economic factors bearing on child labour and to provide a framework for programming. The policy would anticipate the intensification of employment and income generating schemes in area with high incidence of child labour. This calls for specific pilot projects to establish the basis for a larger national progamme of action. This will be implemented directly by Government and non-governmental organisations in the delivery of welfare services and NFE and in raising public awareness.

Child Labour: A Global Estimate

As part of its effort to increase the knowledge base on child labour, the ILO prepared new global estimates on the overall magnitude and distribution of working children. This includes estimates on economically active children, children in child labour that requires elimination and the extent to which children are engaged in hazardous work and other worst forms of child labour.

Children at work in economic activity. It is estimated that there were some 211 million children ages 5 to 14 at work in economic activity in the world in 2000. This accounts for a little less than one-fifth all children in this age group. About 73 million working children are less than 10 years old. The total economically active child population 5-17 years old is estimated at 352 million children. The estimates show that there are no significant gender differences in the global incidence of children at work. In both the (5-9 and 10-14) year age. Boys and girls are equally likely to be engaged in economic activity. Only as boys and girls grow older do we observe a widening gap, with more boys working than girls. A child at work in economic activity is a broad concept that encompasses most productive activities by children, including unpaid and illegal work as well as work in the informal sector. It is, however, not the same as child labour which needs to be eliminated as per the ILO Minimum. Age convention, 1973 (No.138) and the ILO Worst Forms of Child Labour Convention, 1999 (No.182).

Regional Distribution

The Asia-Pacific region labourers, the largest number of child workers in the 5-14 age category, 127.3 million in total. It is followed by Sub-Saharan Africa and Latin America and the Caribbean with 48 million and 17.4 million, respectively. Developed economies and transition economies have the lowest absolute numbers of child workers. Seen in relative terms, Sub-Saharan Africa has the highest proportion of working children. The estimates show that almost one child in three below the age of 15 is economically active in region. The child work ratios in other major world regions are all below 20 per cent. In Asia-Pacific and Latin America and the Caribbean, the incidence is 19 and 16 per cent, respectively. In the Middle East and North Africa, it is 15 per cent.

Table 3.1
Global Estimates of Economically Active Children Ages 5 to 17 in 2000

Age Group	*Total Population ('000s)*	*Number at Work ('000s)*	*Work Ratio (%)*
5-9	600,200	73,100	12.2
10-14	599,200	137,700	23.0
5-14	1,199,400	210,800	17.6
15-17	332,100	140,900	42.4
Total	1,531,100	351,700	23.0

Table 3.2
Regional Estimates of Economically Active Children Ages 5 to 14 in 2000

Region	*Number of Children*	*Work Ratio*
Developed economics	2.5	2
Transition economies	2.4	4
Asia and Pacific	127.3	19
Latin America & Caribbean	17.4	16
Sub-Saharan Africa	48.0	29
Middle East & North Africa	13.4	15
Total	211	18

Child Labour, is a narrower concept than 'economically active children', excluding all those children 12 years and older who are working only a few hours a week in permitted light work and those 15 years and above who work is not classified as 'hazardous'. It is estimated that there were about 186 million child labourers below the age of 15 in the world in 2000. About 110 million were below the age of 12.

Figure 1
CHILD LABOUR
Global Scenario
(In Million)

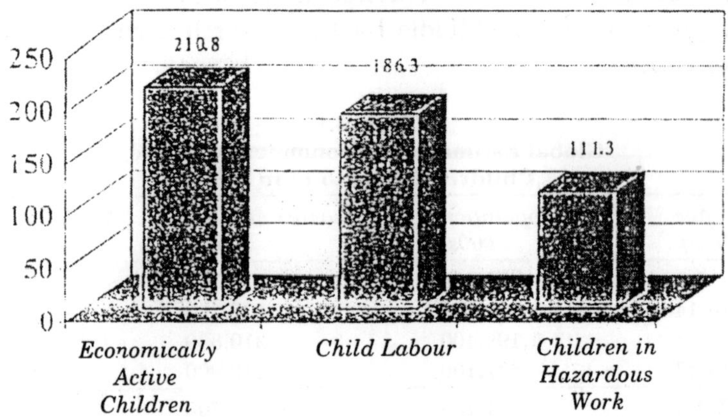

Source: International Labour Organisation, 2002.

Among children in the larger age group 5-17 there approximately 246 million children in child labour. On average, more boys tend to be exposed to child labour than girls, both in absolute as well as in relative terms.

Children in hazardous work. An estimated 111 million children ages 5-17 were estimated to work in hazardous situations or conditions in 2002. In other words, children in hazardous work constituted about half the total number of economically active children and more than two-thirds of those in child labour. A stunning 55 per cent of very young child labourers (i.e. those below 12 years of age) were already working in a hazardous occupation or situation. Boys out number girls in hazardous work across all age groups. Seen in relative terms, among all children about one-half of the working boys were in hazardous situations as compared with a little more than two in five working girls.

Children in unconditional worst forms of child labour. In addition to the number of children in hazardous work, it is estimated that there were about 8.4 million children involved in other worst forms of child labour as defined in ILO Convention No. 182, Art. 3. This in includes trafficking (1.2 million): forced and bonded labour (5.7 million): armed conflict (0.3 million): prostitution and pornography (1.8 million): and illicit activities (0.6 million).

Table 3.3
Estimated Number of Children in Unconditional Worst Forms of Child Labour

Unconditional Worst Form of Child Labour	*Global Estimate ('000s)*
Trafficked Children	1,200
Children in forced and bonded labour	5,700
Children in armed conflict	300
Children in prostitution and pornography	1,800
Children in illicit activities	600
Total	8,400*

* The total excludes the category of trafficked children because of the risk of double-counting.

Chapter - 4

CHILD LABOUR IN INDIA

Child and Child Labour–Magnitude of the Problem

Children are backbone of nation and their health and development is the health of a nation. India has the second largest child population in the world. Their nature and solicitude are our responsibility. It shall be the policy of the state to provide adequate services to children both before and after birth and through the period of growth to ensure their full physically, mental and social development.

Age limits differ from activity to activity and from country to country. Many countries make a distinction between light and hazardous work, with the minimum age for the former generally being twelve, for the latter usually varying between sixteen and eighteen. Generally, almost all the countries accept that maximum age to recognize the young one, as 'Children' is fifteen. The legal definition of 'Child' depends upon the specific legislation enacted for the protection of children.

Status of The Child

Status of children in a country closely depends on its socio-economic conditions and family life styles. It reflects the standard of living in that country. As children are completely dependent on family, society and state for their physical and mental development, they are more vulnerable to the conditions around them. Consequently, the problems faced by the children directly or indirectly influence the national development. They are considered as a part of family and social welfare programmes. Only in the later half of the twentieth century children are recognised as individuals with dignity.

The UN convention on the 'Rights of the Child 1989' treats education as the fundamental right of every child in 5-14 age group and holds that any child in this age group who is out of school should be treated as working child. According to Government of Andhra Pradesh, being out of school is equal to worst form of child labour' hazardous' intolerable, circumstances and 'harmful to the over all growth and development of the child'. As per the 1991 Census, India has a total of population of 297 millions in the 0-14 age group. Of this, children in school-going age i.e. 5-14 constitute 203 millions. Every year 21 million are born, 8 million die, and 13 million survive. Multiplied at this rate 78 million would have been added to 297 million children between 1991-97 totaling 375 million. Similarly, judging by the rate of enrolment, the rate of retention and drop-out and rate of participation of children in the school system (both formal and non-formal), the number of children of school going age (5-14 years) would by now have grown to at least 220 millions. Of this, 112 million go to formal school, about 8 million to non-formal school and the rest i.e. 100 million do not attend school. It is the responsibility of the state to create the infrastructure for facilitating free, compulsory and universal access to both primary and elementary education. There can be no excuse for over 100 million children in the 5-14 age group are being forced to work rather than being sent to school on account of social, economic and cultural compulsions.

Child Labour in India–Magnitude of the Problem

India has the largest number of child labour in the world. According to 1991 census, 11.2 million children in the age group of 5 to 14 are employed in our country. This accounts for 1.35 per cent of the total population, 4 per cent of total working and 3.6 per cent of the total child population of the country. More than 90 per cent of the working children are in rural areas and most of them are employed in agriculture and allied activities. The figures are contradicted by several Non-Governmental Organisations (NGOs) and also do not reflect the complete picture of working children as the census ignores the 'no where children' which is residual category of child population who are neither at school nor reported to be economically active as full time or marginal workers. They are either doing nothing or performing household work not classified as economic activity, and have not been recorded in either of the categories of full time or marginal child labour. Therefore, taking these children into account the NGOs estimates of child labour range from 44 million to 100 million. The Human Development Report (1996) puts the figure of child labour in India anywhere between 14 and 100 million. According to the recent (1999-2000) NSSO (55th round) survey, the number of child labour is 10.4 million.

National Policy for Children in India

The Government of India adopted the resolution on 'National Policy for Children' in 1976 in order to provide better child development and child welfare programmes. The contents of the policy are enunciated below:

1. Equal opportunities for development to all children during the period of growth,
2. To provide better food, shelter and clothing to all children,
3. Right to education to all children,
4. To provide better facilities to all children,
5. To create special conditions to have juvenile justice, liberty etc.

6. To provide adequate resource for child welfare programmes and schemes by the government, and
7. To achieve the above objectives, the State should provide necessary legislative and administrative support.

The government of India is working in this line i.e. to provide food, shelter, clothing, education and protection of human rights of child labour with the help of citizens, local bodies, educational institutions, voluntary organizations etc. in spite of many efforts by the above said agencies to reduce the number of child labour, the problem is going on increasing and it is going to be hurdle to the society in terms of growth. It is due to child labour, dropout children, juvenile delinquents, high-risk children, children needing care and protection etc.

Causes and Consequence of Child Labour: Education and Health

Causes of child labour are many and interrelated. It is not the only one. Is not the possible for classification. However, it may be under following heads: (1) Poverty (2) Family size (3) Economic constrains (4) In adequate school infrastructure (5) Lack of parental motivation (6) Curriculum (7) Caste factor etc.

Millions of children all over the world today are working many in servitude and under hazardous conditions. A large number of children of tender age are being exploited, and compelled to work for long hours for low wages and under conditions damaging to their health, and to their physical, social, psychological and mental development. Millions of children are thus being deprived of their healthy childhood.

When children work, both their education and health suffer. How does this happen? The Indian school system has a single point entry and consists of a sequential and full-time format of institutional instruction by full time and professional teachers. One of the most comprehensive critiques of such a system in relation to the circumstances and needs of rural and agriculture society has been for formulated by the noted educationist, the late J.P. Naik. He argues for a radical transformation in the traditional model of formal education. Naik makes a number constructive suggestion to orient the school system to the needs of rural working children. For one thing, the school calendar should be so adjusted as to allow time off for agricultural operation like sowing and harvesting; for another, to reduce stagnation on account of children failing examinations, flexible systems which condense the curricula of classes I to IV into a shorter period of about two years for children over eleven could be devised. Another important recommendation he makes is to have pre-schools or crèches attached to primary schools so that girls could bring their younger siblings there and look after them, as well as get an education. Instead of relying upon full time professional teachers who raise the costs of the school system. Naik suggests simple solutions like employing local carpenters, tailors, singers and young persons who could teach for part of the time. Such a step would also generate additional local employment a lower cost. In summary, Naik's contribution has been to suggest that the school system be re-oriented to cater to the needs of working children in a agricultural society, in a practicable way and, at a low cost.

The lack of adequate infrastructure apart, the most common explanation for parents not sending their children to school is that they are too poor. It is argued that the economic contribution of the child to the income of the family-where by bringing in a wage or by doing household maintenance work and thus, adults for productive work-it so important that the family cannot afford to lose this economically productive time for his or her schooling. Clearly, there is some substance in such reasoning, as poor families exist on the margins, of survival.

Working children in India, by and large, belong to the poor regions of the country, the socially disadvantaged sections of society and some minority groups. There is a vested interest in seeing that the children of the poor do not avail themselves of the facilities for education.

Glass Bias in Education

It is demonstrable that children who work belong to the lowest strata of society and children who stay out school also belong to the lowest rung in the class structure.

According to the Acharya, more than 92 per cent of one set of respondents who were lower middle and poor peasants as also agricultural laborers replied to the relevant question by saying that their non-enrolled children were either gainfully employed or did household work during school hours.

Acharya makes an important statement regarding the attitude of the upper strata society towards free compulsory education. He explains the oppositions towards making elementary education compulsory by referring to the fear of the jotedars and the rich peasants that the traditional order would be disturbed. He observes that the continuing illiteracy of the labouring groups helps the reinforcement of the traditional patterns of authority in village's life.

Acharya's study found that the rich peasant did not want compulsory education it would be inconvenient for them although all the children of the jotedars in the age group six to eleven years and 84 per cent of the children of the rich peasants of the same age-group were enrolled. Acharya does not mince words when he says:

"The reasons are very simple. They are against compulsion as they fear that universal and compulsory enrolment would deprive them of the easy supply of child labour. In that case, they would need to hire adults at a higher wage instead of child labour, which would lead to an increase in their cost of agricultural production."

Other studies are also pointers to local vested interests who do not want the children of the poor to get an education. The Rural wing of the National Labour Institute conducted a study on bonded labour. Investigators interviewed some owners of bonded labourers in Andhra Pradesh about education for working children, their response was:

Once they are allowed to come up to an equal level, nobody will go to the fields. Fields will be left uncultivated everywhere. We have to keep them under our strong thumb in order to get work done (NLI Rural Wing, 1977).

As in the case of unorganised industry, they cases cited above from backward sectors of the agricultural economy bring out the importance of the need of upper segments of the population to maintain illiteracy and thereby their hold on a docile and submissive labour force. When one studies the links between child labour and education, it is helpful to remember the social contexts in which child labour flourishes at the expense of the education. The working child suffers from the spiraling disadvantages of being illiterate, coming from economically poor classes and belonging to socially backward communities.

Working Children and Schools

There is point of view frequently propounded by professionals in the field of education and policy makers that the existing school system is irrelevant to the needs of working children. It is argued that sterile curricula, rote-based learning and the poor quality of teachers, amongst others ills, plague he school system and that, therefore, neither the parents of working children nor the children themselves are keen to gain access to it.

Education alone can provide mobility to the socially and economically disadvantaged sections of society. More correctly it is straightened economic circumstances which prevent the fulfillment of this aspiration; inadequate school infrastructure tilts the balance in favour of work.

Where the economic circumstances of the worker improved because of some reason or the other, the first thing they did was to remove their children from the work force and put them into school even if they substituted them with children of an even poorer group. It would seem to be a myth, sometimes sedulously cultivated, that poor parents are simply not interested in a formal education for their children. In every industry workers knew about how section of the better off, like the entrepreneur, the trader and the exporter, send their children to school to learn English so that they would be able to deal better with the outside world.

Impact of Health

It is ironical that the conservative approaches of experts have grown with fresh information regarding the deleterious effects of work on the health of young children. Many discussions on health hazards for working children start with opening statements like; "Not all work is hazardous to children" (Gore 1985) or 'work' can in fact be beneficial to the child (Pit 1985a). More recently, an important study conducted in Mumbai has argued that working children are in fact healthier than non-working children are in fact because of the food get to eat. In fairness, it must also be said that those who have written extensively about health hazards to working children and have argued that not all work is harmful (Pitt, 1985a) have also admitted that not enough information is available on the subject.

By the large children who are examined at the work-site are amongst the fittest. What about those who have fallen by the way side-injured or ill or even dead as a result of overwork, exhaustion and so on? To leave them out of the count is to be unscientific and leads to a distorted version of the facts. Such selectivity leads to what may be termed the 'pragmatic' view increasingly favoured these days by experts. This pragmatism bodes ill for the vision of health as a fundamental human right.

A different type of hazards faced by working children and proposes a scheme of classification for them. Firstly, children are employed in intrinsically hazardous occupations where they may contract silicosis, pneumoconiosis, byssinosis, etc., by working in the slate, rock, glass and power loom industries. Secondly, some hazards find their origin in the poor working environment. Thirdly, a few occupations may be considered safe but the vulnerability of children makes these occupations hazardous for them. Hence, one has to examine (a) whether hazards are intrinsic to the nature of the work itself, or (b) whether they arise from the working environment and conditions of work, or (c) whether the work is simply unsuitable for children.

Any occupation which allows the workers to come into contact with harmful substances like chemicals (as in the balloon, match and fire-works, lock and brass ware industries) or fire (as in the glass industry) or cotton fluff and dust that damage the lungs (as in the power loom industry) may be termed intrinsically hazardous. These occupations would be hazardous for all workers, both adults and children. But since children are still in the process of growing and attaining their full physical stature, their growth is likely to be affected.

Child Labour in Rural India

Although it is difficult to assess the magnitude of child labour in India, the population Census provides data on the extent of child labour with ten-year intervals for all the census years i.e. 1961, 1971, 1981, 1991 and 2001. The data from the National Sample Survey and Rural Labour Enquiry are available for different years and do not exactly coincide with Population Census years. The Population Census provides figures of the total population and working population by age group including the age group 0-14 years. The total population is divided into workers and non-workers and the working population is further sub-divided by age of the workers. The distribution of the population and workers by age enables us to estimate the absolute numbers of working children and the percentage of working children in the total children population aged between 10-143 years. In the Census of 1961 and 1971 the data on ages of workers are provided for workers in general where as in 1981 and 1991, the workers were sub-divided into main workers and marginal workers.

Another important source on child labour data is the National Sample Survey (NSS). The third official source on child labour is the Rural Labour Enquiry Survey (RELS). The data from RELS are generated from the National Sample Survey. Therefore the period of RELS correspond with that of the NSS. However, the information in the Rural Labour Enquiry concerns only rural areas and rural labour households.

Since about 75 per cent of India's population lives in rural areas, it is not surprising to find majority of child labour in these areas.

Census data from 1991 show that about 80 per cent of the child labourers' work in the agricultural sector. Among the male child workers 78 per cent is engaged in this sector, among the female workers this is 83 per cent. This means that overall female children are more involved in low paid jobs than male children. When comparing these numbers with the figures from 1961, it can be seen that there is a sharp decline in children working in cultivation and a sharp increase in children working as agricultural labourers. This indicates more and more pauperization of rural masses depending on agriculture.

According to Chaudri & Wilson (2000), the estimated child population (6-14 years) is 175.9 million and 85.8 per cent of them are in rural areas and 14.4 per cent in urban areas. The large number of children in rural areas also reflects in more number of child workers. Some children 8.9 million children are estimated to be engaged in full-time child labour, 90.9 per cent of these were in rural areas and only 9.1 per cent in urban areas. Of this 90.9 per cent, 74.4 per cent were employed in the rural agricultural sector and 16.6 per cent in the rural non-agricultural sector (village industries, service sectors, etc.).

In 1961, 14.6 per cent of the children below the age of 14 were found working in rural India with a range of only 2.2 per cent in Kerala and 15.6 per cent in Rajasthan. States with low incidence of rural male child labour were Kerala, West Bengal, Gujarat, Uttar Pradesh, Punjab and Haryana. In 1971, it declined everywhere except in Karnataka and Andhra Pradesh. In 1981 Census, Andhra Pradesh is the only state where more than 10 per cent of rural male children were working. The pattern observed in 1991 suggested lowest incidence of rural male child labour in Kerala, Haryana, Himachal Pradesh and Uttar Pradesh while the highest was in Andhra Pradesh, Karnataka and Madhya Pradesh.

Incidence of rural female child labour in 1961 had a marked regional bias. Rajasthan, Madhya Pradesh, Andhra Pradesh and Himachal Pradesh had extremely high incidence of rural female workers while Kerala, Uttar Pradesh, Punjab, Haryana and West Bengal had low incidence. The change in definition of term 'worker' in 1971 affected rural female workers much more than others. Therefore, 1961 and 1971 Census data are not strictly compared. A proper comparison would be between 1971, 1981 and 1991 Census. Analysis of these data clearly suggests that the incidence of rural female child labour has worsened in the states like Andhra Pradesh, Karnataka, Madhya Pradesh between 1971 to 1991. The highest incidence being 12 per cent in Andhra Pradesh against an all India average of 4.4 per cent.

In summary, the sectoral distribution of rural full time child labour indicates that that of 8.9 million 74.4 per cent are in the rural agricultural sector and 16.6 per cent in the rural non agricultural sector (village industries, services sectors etc). In the category of 'Nowhere' children (children who are neither in school nor in labour but who are supposed to doing some work, either paid or unpaid, within or outside the family) 93.6 per cent were in rural areas. This means "child labour and nowhere children are largely rural phenomena".

Socio-Economic and Gender Dimensions of Child Labour in India

The Problem of child labourers in centuries old and has allowed socio-economic attention and protection. Prevalence of child labour is more or less seen in all periods of time and it varies in nature and dimension depending on the existing socio-economic structure of society. We must be aware that children of today are like the potential buds which would blossom into the fragrant flowers of tomorrow. They need to be given social and economic protection if a country is to thrive and prosper in all spheres of human activity. Paradoxically, it is unfortunate to say that tragically most of the child life is lost poverty, destitution, malnutrition and poor and unhygienic conditions, largely in the rural sector compared to the urban counter part.

Historically, in our country child labour has been seen as an economic phenomenon. The relationship between children and work is dictated to a great extent by the stage of economic development or the system of production prevalent in a country, consequently a change in the economic system or the mode of production brings a change in the structure of the labour force and correspondingly a change in the economic role of children. Thus, with the onset of industrialisation and the prospect of wage labour, children have become progressively employed in industry as well as domestic and commercial establishments.

So far, child labour has been accepted because it is believed to have an economic basis that fits into a demand/ supply framework. On the demand side there are two sets of reasons why employers prefer to use children. Employing children is a cheaper and more stable proposition and hence a more profitable one. Children can be employed at much lower wages than adults and made to work longer hours. The piece rate system or remuneration that is the norm with child labour benefits only the employers. Children do not form unions, they are less likely to change jobs quickly, a the same time, they can be easily laid off should the need arise without any form of compensation. The other reasons why there exists a demand for children which lend themselves to employment in certain industries. In general children are considered "more active, agile and quick and feel less tired than adults in certain jobs". Also they can be admonished, pulled up and punished for faults without jeopardizing relations. (Quoted from Kiran Bhatty).

On the supply side, the most commonly cited explanation given for child labour is the poverty of households that supply children to the labour force. The perceptions that exist towards children and work are dictated by the low economic status of families where children are seen as economic assets. It is contended that families of working children are so poor that their very survival is threatened thus children are in various activities including working as family labour in household enterprise, assisting in contracts undertaken by parents, taking over various household duties to enable parents to do other work and working outside the home as cheap labour in small factories, commercial and domestic establishments. The cost category often forces them to spend large amounts of time away from their homes working in conditions not conducive to their health and safety. Not only do the children earn their own livelihood and often that of others as well, they allow parents to spend more time on income generating work by taking charge of household duties. Greater importance is given to the learning of skills from an early age, as opposed to school education as it is believed that school curricula detach children from the village economy, creating aspirations for white collar jobs that are hard to get. The skills on the other hand will enable them in securing employment in their adult life. Thus child labour is considered as a kind of apprenticeship and perceived as a vital part of the learning process and in no way detrimental to the child's development and finally the quality of the schools (those that exists at all) is so poor that parents have to be induced to send their children to them and children are not motivated to attend either. Hence, it appears that the overall economic situation coupled with a lack of proper educational facilities perpetuates the persistence of child labour.

(a) Socio-Economic Analysis

The socio-economic structure of the working class promotes increasing involvement of the child labour force. Different modes of exploitation and unhealthy working conditions has resulted in their plight. They are ill-fed, ill-clad and ill-housed. Illiteracy, unemployment, poverty, population pressure, family disorganisation due to divorce, loss of parents are the important causes of emergence of child labour. A Survey Report of the Directorate of Labour and Employment, Government of Orissa, reveals that due to poverty factor the percentage of male child labour is 17.44 per cent and female child labour is 20 per cent for female child labour. The corresponding figure for male and female child labour due to death of parents is 4.10 per cent and 10 per cent. Since 94.86 per cent of child labour is Orissa come from the rural areas, the growth of child labour due to illiteracy is 8.20 per cent. In the metropolitan cities and big towns, growth of urban slums as reflection of poverty originates the child labour force.

It is unwillingly done because of the compulsion of economic distress and it remains a universal truth in all classes of the society. There is, 'poverty within poverty'. The economically backward people have gained a little within backward regions. Both economically and socially they were, kept outside the circumference of the development scheme. Economics poverty, social segregation and oppression continues. The poorest become the first-casualty in the event of natural and human made calamities.

The residential distribution of child workers show that about 4/5th, of them are of rural origin. Labourers migrate from rural areas to urban centers because migrate labourers are economically better of in urban area then their counterparts in the villages. Non-availability of opportunity to work and craze for better earnings induce the parents as well as the children to migrate to urban areas. Higher dependency ratio i.e., of non-earning to earning members compel the children to offer themselves in any occupation they find suitable or not.

An observation of the caste background shows that more than three-fourth of the children workers belong backward caste. In fact, there is high degree of correlation between caste and economic position. Illiteracy and low educational standard is of the same time both the cause and consequence of child labour. When their parents prefer their child earning to learning.

A study of the informal sector shows that 86 per cent of child workers belong to backward castes and also 86 per cent of them are between 11 to 14 years of age and one-third of the family heads of child workers are illiterate.

(b) Working Conditions and Living Standard

Child workers are not only ill-paid or under paid but also are victims all treatment and in human conditions of work. They continue deplorable state with economic and social misery with no hope of amelioration are betterment of their lot. Then ILO remarked that they are unorganised and it is due to their existence that the organise workers have weak bargaining power. When the labour market overloaded with cheap child labour, the capitalist method of exploitative practices is being aggravated. Small entrepreneurs are eager to employ large proportion of child labour is they demand for wage and bargaining power is less and suit the best to the cold interest of capitalist. The terms and conditioned of employment, security of employment, hours of work, amount of wages paid, severity of the work given very often amount violate the usual labour legislation, precisely due to the weakness of the working force. Casual workers are deprived of their right full economic and working concessions. They suffer from health hazards enough noise, dust, ill-ventilation etc. create hart and lung disease, loss of eye site etc. The working environment not only in congenial, but also unsafe. The wage paid of the child worker are generally 30 per cent to 50 per cent of the wages of the adult. They are also not given adequate rest and largely employed in contract basis. Is it not a pity to see a child of 12 or 13 carrying to heavy to tin pull of water on his shoulder for 15 paisa Rs. 1.00 one in a hotel or canteen? Does his muscle permit show? There are not only economic but also human questions before the employers, the government authorities and the society at large. Is it not the plight of child of 12 to 14 years rickshaw carrying a passenger and luggage load of 4 to 5 quintals for Rs. 5.00 or Rs. 10.00 all are passive onlookers of the plight? It is not rate to find a child labour working as hotel boy and eating and the residual food of the customers of the waste of the canteen which is highly and unhygienic.

Income earned by the child workers is substantially low. The amount of wages paid is not only meager but also irregular. The child workers make desperate efforts to support their family. Average monthly earnings per workers varies between Rs. 150 to Rs. 300. In the unorganised non-industrial sectors they are sometimes provided with food and dress. However, the fact remains they are ill-fed, ill-clad and ill-housed. They largely live in the rural and tribal hunts and in urban slums in the small tenants, those lack adequate space and ventilation. So their living and housing condition is equally miserable. Large mass of rural migrant labourers is the developing cities find their accommodation in the huts of slum settlements. A great majority of more than two-thirds of the workers support their families which shows a formidable association between poverty and child labour.

The living condition of the child labour show that they are socially neglected economically exploited and morally tortured. Girl children engaged in domestic works and in industries are morally under the pressure of economic circumstances.

According to an International Labour Organisation study, additionally some 50 million children under the age of 15 years of age supplement income for their struggling families in India.

Thousands of minor girls perform unpaid household jobs, facing problems ranging from eve teasing to rape, which rage unabated, and all abuse there are no laws designed to effectively protect them. The lack of education and other alternative avenues for financial security have forced children into prostitution (some estimates put the number of child prostitutes at a whopping figure of four lakhs). Sheer apathy or lack of will on the part of law enforcing agencies has only aggravated the problems.

Child labour is the work by children which interferes with their full physical development and their opportunities for a desirable minimum of education and recreation. It is an unhealthy economic practice and social evil. In economic sense employment of children in gainful occupation add to the income of the family and in the social aspect it takes into account the damages to which children are exposed which means the denial of opportunities for development. Child labour has social aspect and economic implications. Child labour exerts a negative effect on child health. It seriously interferes with the education and precludes the most productive participation in the privileges and obligation of citizens. It is the economic backwardness which pushes the child or the infants to toil for their bread. The problem of child labour is extended to child beggary and boded labour. Disturbs the emotional ties between the children and their parents which is turned into a commercial interaction. Child labour involves the use of labour at lowest productivity, they are necessarily handicapped by limitation of physical strength and are thrown to situation physically and morally exploitations.

Hence, child labour is economically unsound, psychologically disastrous and physically as well as morally dangerous and harmful. It is imperative for eradication of employment and exploitation of child labour.

(c) Policy Imperatives

The problem and evil practice of child labour should be doubly attacked. On the hand, the income of the poorer section of the people should be increased and on the other prohibition of child labour should be strictly followed. Hence, policy options in both preventive and curative aspect.

The Committee on Child Welfare suggested that the nature and intensity of child workers in various occupations has to be careful studied and policy by framed to root out the unhealthy practice. Central and State Level Advisory Committee be formed to have vigilant eye on the problem.

The Directive Principles of State Policy embodied in the Constitution of India reaffirm the policy of protection of children against exploitation. The state shall in particular direct its policy towards securing that the health and strength of workers, men and women and the tender age children are not abused and that citizens are not force by economic necessity to enter a vocation unhealthy to their age and strength, that childhood and youth are protected against exploitation and against moral and material abandonment. The National Human Rights Commission has suggested measures for collection of statistics of child labour and their rehabilitation as a humanitarian issue.

Eradication of the problem of child labour calls for a long term or 'Perspective. Action Plan'. Their social and economic requirements should not be undennined by the Government with the felling that they are not voters. The Child Welfare Council has been functioning since 1982 under the Ministry of Labour Welfare. Child labour is global problem and its needs dedication of the Government authorities and construction of a special forum to have better integration with the Non-Government Organisations (NGOs). Child labour is the outcome of our social and economic system the solution of which requires a co-ordinate effort. Mere provision of legislative or constitutional measures is not the answer to the problem. It requires as strong political will to cure this social cancer. The International Agreement, 1989 emphasised upon the protection and growth of children. Other steps in this regard are the Sanat Mehta Committee 1980, Gurupada Swamy Committee 1979. The Orissa Child Labour (prohibition and regulation) Rules, etc.

The I.L.O. 'Report on the Protection of Children and Young workers' has rightly emphasised "the problem of prohibition of child labour" is nextricably mixed-up with the problem of the maintenance of the child and the provision of a living wage for all employed persons adequate to maintain the family at an adequate standard. The committee on child welfare stressed on minimum age of entry into any field of employment as fifteen, minimum age of entry into any field of employment as fifteen, minimum educational qualification of 8th standard, suitable arrangement for non-formal education, implementation of specific health schemes for parents in areas of concentration of working children, strengthening the existing machinery for enforcement of legislation relating to employment of children and due recognition to the role of voluntary agencies and trade unions.

Since in India widespread, prevalence of child labour can be attributed to poverty, child labour cannot be eliminated in the presence of poverty and starvation. While child labour emerges due to economic necessity protection of children can be made by providing sufficient income to the parents of child labour. A pressing obligation in this regard is to put on wage payment, on adequate basis.

Free and compulsory education should be given highest priority. The Gurupada Swamy Committee reported that the "major concern of the Government should be in regard to evolving a meaningful policy for education of these children."

The I.L.O. suggested employ children between 15-18 to do light work not harmful to health and development; provided it did not interfere with the education. Employment of children is indeed more of an economic problem than any thing, else. While economic difficulties are real, a way is to find out to give the child necessary education in his more receptive years. It is a feeling of sympathy rather than desire to exploit that weighs much as a suggestive measure. Integration of work with education should be pragmatic keeping in view the future prospect of the child. It will create a skilled man power. So, special free education, subsidised food and improvement of health are the needs of the hour. For this greater involvement of the administrative authorities is essential. The child labour continues as a soldier in the battle of life. Whenever, necessary the children should not be allowed to work beyond 4 to 5 hours and the residual time should be diverted to education and play. A National Policy on labour is needed for. Target has been kept to completely abolish the practice by the end of 2000 A.D. The proper place of children is the school and not the work place. Charitable Trusts should provide social security by nursing them.

Voluntary efforts need to strengthened. There should be a radical change in the manner in which the bureaucracy deals with voluntary organisations. An extension oriented promotive style of functioning is very important to accomplish the objectives. Programmes of voluntary organisations must be documented and widely disseminated so that the society is in a better position to assess their endeavours. The problem these child, workers deserves special consideration, sympathy and speedy action. Since it is a socio-economic and legal problem, it is high time for Government, voluntary organisations, social workers, thinkers and policy-makers, as a whole to provide a suitable alternative to them. To take care of these child workers remaining in malnutrition. Physically and mentally tortured and suffering from various diseases, there should be a community level approach to start dormitory type residential schools, where besides free education, they should be provided free food, health facilities, clothes and emotional support. They should be given some vocational training to make some material goods like soap, rope, basket, dons etc., but not at cost of their education. They require much more than a few rupees. It requires organised efforts.

Integrated Child Development Scheme need to be strengthened in rural and urban areas. A National Policy for children was adopted in August, 1974 which recoganised that the "nations children are a supreme important asset". The identified programme include includes "Prevention and Promotive aspect of child health, nutrition for infants, maintenance education and training of orphan destitute and handicapped children". It laid the foundations for proper psychological physical and social development. Hence, what is required is a 'package of services' as education, health, social security and employment guarantee of the parents of the child workers?

In India, general improvement of economic and social conditions of people will result in eliminating gradually the child labour from the industry largely in the unorganised sector. An improvement of the standard of living will prevent the poverty-stricken parents from relying on the earnings of their children. Hence, total abolition of child labour through legislation may not be feasible or desirable in the foreseeable future. There is an apprehension that such a step may dislocate the industrial structure and cause widespread economic distress. Hence, the appropriate alternative policy is to improve the employment and working conditions and living standards of the children employed in the informal sectors to save them from ruthless and inhuman exploitation by the employers and groups of vested interests.

The I.L.O. in pursuit of Labour Welfare reaffirmed that labour is not a commodity. There must be provision of assuring equality of educational and vocational opportunity. Hence, policy changes are called for relating to age and conditions of employment, referral services, hours of work, earnings to provide the minimum needs and protection and preparing an army efficient and productive labour force in the future. It is a new orientation to manpower planning.

The employment of children is product of action and interaction of numerous subjective and object factors. Economic structure of the families vital in participation of children in the labour market. In human exploitation of children for the sake of earnings their livelihood cannot be compromised. Legislation solution can only be a partial remedy this can be taken care of by an action group of trade unions those agitate for the children's right. Subjective benevolent intentions and endeavours can hardly solve the problem of child labour. It is a challenge before the working class to establish their due recognition in the society in a democratic and progressive state.

Labour Welfare is not charity before the employers. It is an economic, social, moral and human claim by the working class. An integration of economic and social change will provide the suitable solution to the problem.

Chapter - 5

ECONOMIC ROLE OF CHILDREN IN INDIA AND ITS STATES

Child Labour Situation in India

Child labour is undeniably a part of the workforce both in the organised and the unorganised sectors of the Indian economy. The country holds the dubious distinction of having the highest concentration of child labour in the work with the estimates ranging from 10 million (Government) to 100 million (NGOs/TUs). The reason for large variation in the estimates of child labour between government and non-government sources lies mainly in the criteria adopted for the identification of child labour.

Census is the major source of information utilised by researchers dealing with child labour, as it is the only source, which provides comparable data as also distribution of workers, by sex, residence and activity. Indian Census has not been the same over the time. For instance, there were substantial differences in the definition of the 'worker' in 1961 and 1971 and the change in definition has mostly affected worm and children. In the 1991 Census, a person was counted as a 'worker' if he or she had some regular work of more than one hour per day through out the greater part of the working season in case of person engaged I seasonal work like cultivation, livestock, dairying, household industry, etc. As a result of this definition of worker, a large number of persons, especially women and children became a worker even if they were only marginally related with the work force.

Because of his criticism of the 1961 Census definition of worker, emphasis was placed in the 1971 Census on the main activity of each individual, that is how each person was mostly engaged as a worker or non-worker. That person was defined as a worker whose main activity was participation in an economically productive work by his physical and mental activity. Work included not only actual work but also effective supervision or direction of work. The effect of the above change in the definition of worker between the 1961 and 1971 Census was the exclusion of all those person who were only marginally connected with economic activity. The number of child workers below the age of 15 declined from 14.5 million in 1961 to 10.8 million in 1971. This decline was observed in case of both males and females (Premi-1994). According to the Census of India, 1981, there are 263 million children aged fourteen years or under comprising 39.5 per cent of the total population of the country Approximately, 11.2 million children are notified as main workers.

The country holds the dubious distinction of having the highest concentration of child labour in the world. The 1991 Census estimated 11.2 million workers (including marginal workers) in India below the age of 14 years. According to the 50th round of the National Sample Survey conducted in 1993-94, the child labour was estimated to be 8.9 million out of which 90.9 per cent (8.1 million) lived in rural areas and 9.1 per cent (0.8 million) in urban areas. However, the estimates from various non-governmental sources put this number much higher ranging from 44 to 100 million. The reason for large variation in the estimates of child labour between government and non-government sources lies mainly in the criteria adopted for the identification of child labour. The NSSO, 50th rounds furnishes us information on employment of children working in specific hazardous occupation in manufacturing at the country level. Nearly 7 per cent of the child workers in rural areas and about 24 per cent in urban areas worked in these dangerous industries in 1993-94. Two industries, cloth painting/dyeing and weaving and bidi rolling which employed both boys and girls are identified as the most hazardous in rural as well as urban areas (Thorat, 1999). The working children aged 11-15 years were mainly from lower economic background in carpet industries. The child labour in these industries was mostly illiterate. They generally belonged to backward and scheduled castes. Despite working more than 11 hours per day they earned an average of Rs.145 per month. They found that abolition of child labour was not favoured either by parents or employers because of economic reasons (Singh-1990). The estimated number of working children in the country the as per the 55th Round of the NSSO Survey (1999-2000) is 10.40 million. Table 5.1 exhibits the incidence of child labour in the major states in India. In all the States,

Table 5.1
Incidence of Child Labour in India*–1991

States	*Male*	*Female*	*Total*
Andhra Pradesh	4.18	7.72	5.40
Assam	3.39	5.09	3.72
Bihar	2.73	5.08	3.10
Gujarat	2.16	4.67	2.65
Haryana	1.63	4.28	1.89
Himachal Pradesh	1.07	3.44	1.73
Karnataka	3.76	7.12	4.73
Kerala	0.25	0.65	0.34
Madhya Pradesh	3.26	5.80	4.00
Maharashtra	1.91	4.04	2.60
Orissa	2.57	5.66	3.13
Punjab	2.09	3.87	2.17
Rajasthan	2.47	7.84	3.53
Tamil Nadu	1.71	3.64	2.29
Uttar Pradesh	2.51	4.73	2.77
West Bengal	2.46	5.81	2.88
India	2.55	5.32	3.18

* Refers to percentage of main child workers to total main workers– 1991 Census.

the Incidence of female child labour is high vis-a-vis male child labour, highlighting the gender discrimination prevalent in the society.

This Sectoral Allocation of total child labour is presented in Table 5.2. The data reveals about 79.1 per cent of the child workers belong to Agriculture sectors, which is out of Child Labour Act (1986). The proportion of manufacturing sectors was only 3.3 per cent in 1991. If we want to really reduce to child labour in this country, send children to schools.

Table 5.3 depicts the distribution of children in various categories. Though the phenomenon of 'Nowhere Children' (children neither in school nor at work) has been on a decline, the total number of children in this category continues to be very high (43.9 per cent in 1991). The proportion of children who arc ncither in schools not in labour force, we have been called 'Nowhere Children', declined from 71.7 per cent to 31.9 per cent for boys and from 75.9 per cent to 42.6 per cent for girls (Chaudhari-2000). The Government should bring these children within the fold of education. Making primary education compulsory could be a step in the right direction. Moreover, there have been numerous studies in the field of child labour that have brought out a strong negative correlation between education and child labour. Myron Weiner (1991) had aptly identified the issue of the failure of the state is providing school education. He stated, "less that half of India's children between ages six and fourteen (82.2 million) are not school. They stay at home to care for cattle, tend younger children collect firewood and work in the fields. They find employment in cottage industries, tea stalls, restaurants, or as household workers in middle class homes. They become prostitutes or live as street children, begging or picking rags and bottles from trash for resale. Many are bonded labourers and working as agricultural labourers for local landowners. India's policy-makers have not regarded mass education as essential to India's modernisation."

Table 5.2
Sector wise Allocation of Child Labour in India (1981-91)

Sl. No.	Particulars	Census Year			
		1981		1991	
		Million	Per cent	Million	Per cent
1.	Total Child labour	11.1	100.00	9.1	100
2.	Cultivators	4.0	36.0	3.2	35.1
3.	Agricultural	4.7	42.4	4.0	44.0
4.	Manufacturing	0.4	3.6	0.3	3.35.
5.	Others	2.0	18.0	1.6	17.6

Source: Census of India, 1981 and 1991. Data cited in D.P. Chaudhari (1997)

Table 5.3
Distribution of Children (5-14 years) in India (1961-1991)

	Category	Numbers	Per cent
	Students	34,595,761	30.4
1961	Child Labour	14,469,775	12.7
	Nowhere	64,914,608	57.0
	Total	113.9 million	100
	Category	*Numbers*	*Per cent*
	Students	50,692,063	33.6
1971	Child Labour	10,664,018	7.1
	Nowhere	89,482,128	59.3
	Total	150.8 million	100
	Category	*Number*	*Per cent*
	Students	78,860,388	43.9
1981	Child Labour	11,195,542	6.2
	Marginal Workers	87,095,986	48.5
	Nowhere	2,445,329	1.4
	Total	179.5 million	100
	Category	*Numbers*	*Per cent*
	Students	106,402,142	50.7
1991	Child Labour	9,110,354	4.3
	Marginal Workers	92,273,392	43.9
	Nowhere	2,200,742	1.0
	Total	209.9 million	100

* Main Workers
Source: Census of India, 1961, 1971, 1981 and 1991.

Child Deprivation: Trends and Composition–in Andhra Pradesh

The phenomenon of child deprivation is a harsh reality, especially in India. While locating the causal relationship, wide rage of factors out economic, demographic, socio-cultural and political dimensions have been brought to the forefront. The phenomenon of child deprivation is said to be a demand-side problem which implies that children are not attending schools because they working. It indicates the opportunity cost of schooling in the realm of poverty and economic necessities. What is missing is the supply side aspect: children are working because they are not attending school. Here the causation runs in reverse direction: lack of availability, access, unsatisfactory quality and high cost of schooling keeps the children out of school. In either case of demand and supply, children fall into the realm of work. Therefore, it is presumed that all out of school children work either due to economic compulsions or lack of alternatives i.e. schooling. Even if they are not working for the moment, they are potential workers. Children work in different forms.

In Andhra Pradesh it was found that in 1961 a little over one-fourth of the total populations were children in the age groups 5-14 years. In the decades of sixties and seventies, the share went up by one percentage point and by 1991 declined to about 25 per cent once again. The shares of child population from the SCs and STs were slightly higher than the 'Other' population both in 1981 and 1991.

The data presented in Table 5.2 shows that there was a high incidence of child deprivation over the period. It is observed that in 1961 the incidence of total deprived children was above 72 per cent. However, by 1991 it came down to 50 per cent.

All throughout the educational deprivation was higher for the rural children compared with their urban counterparts. The incidence of deprivation for rural children was close to 77 per cent in 1961 and 56.2 per cent by 1991. While that for urban children it was 51 per cent in 1961 and 34 per cent in 1991.

Table 5.4
Percentage of Deprived Children to total Child Population by Gender and Location: Andhra Pradesh, 1961-91

Year	*Rural and Urban*			*Rural*			*Urban*		
	All	*Male*	*Female*	*All*	*Male*	*Female*	*All*	*Male*	*Female*
1	2	3	4	5	6	7	8	9	10
1961	72.3	64.1	80.7	76.9	69.0	84.9	51.2	42.0	60.9
1971	72.7	66.1	79.1	78.4	71.7	85.3	48.2	42.7	54.1
1981	59.5	51.3	68.0	66.5	57.5	75.8	35.8	30.2	41.5
1991	50.2	43.8	56.9	56.2	48.6	64.3	33.6	30.7	36.6

Source: Census of India (1991) Working children, RGI, New Delhi

Tabel 5.5
Differences is Child Deprivation by Location and Gender: Andhra Pradesh

	Female to Male			*Rural to Urban*		
Year	*Total*	*Rural*	*Urban*	*All*	*Male*	*Female*
1	2	3	4	5	6	7
1961	16.6	15.9	18.9	25.7	27.0	24.0
1971	13.0	13.6	11.4	30.2	29.0	31.2
1981	16.7	18.3	11.3	30.7	27.3	34.3
1991	13.1	15.7	5.9	22.6	17.9	27.7

Note: 1. Gender Diff. = F-M and Location Diff. = R-U
2. Data presented in differences in percentage points.

Source: Computed from Table 5.2 above.

It is important observe that deprivation was more among female children than their male counterparts. Though the percentage of deprived children had come down over the period, the percentage of deprived female children remained high. This phenomenon was found to be more strikingly visible in the rural areas as compared to the urban areas. It is all more clear form the Table 5.3. There is a clear evidence to show that in urban areas the difference in the share of deprived, between boys and girls had been narrowing down but it was not the case for the rural children.

Child Labour Situation in Andhra Pradesh

As per 1981 and 1991 population census reports Andhra Pradesh had the highest incidence of child labour in the country. About 15 per cent of all child workers in the country were concentrated in A.P. Work participation rate of children (5-14) in A.P. during 1991 was 10 per cent while it was around 5 per cent for the country as a whole. Within AP Mahbubnagar, Kurnool and Guntur account for account for higher concentration of child workers than the state average. Work participation rate of children (5-14) in Mahbubnagar, Kumool and Guntur were 14.1, 13.6 and 11.2 per cent respectively. A Survey conducted during mid-90s by DPEP programme estimated that there were 150,000 in the age group of 5-14 in the workforce in Kurnool district. Another important aspect of children in this district is the significant number of children who are neither in work nor in school did (These children term as 'nowhere children'). In Mahboobnagar, Kurnool and Guntur, the proportion of 'nowhere children' were 52.8, 48.1 and 37.3 per cent respectively of the children in the age group of 5-14 years during 1991. These districts being predominantly rural, most of these 'nowhere children' were in the rural areas. Though they are not categorised as child workers, these children are vulnerable to work related exploitation.

As per the 1991 census child workers are mainly concentrated in Mahaboobnagar and Karimnagar districts of Telangana region, Guntur, West Godavari and Krishna district of Andhra region and Kurnool and Anantapur district of Rayalaseema region (See Table 5.6).

Table 5.6
Incidence of Child Labour in Andhra Pradesh–District wise

Sl. No.	*Name of the District*	*Male*	*%*	*Female*	*%*	*Total*	*%*
1.	Srikakulam	27,280	3.4	32,675	3.8	59,955	3.6
2.	Vizianagaram	31,377	3.9	31,250	3.7	62,627	3.8
3.	Vishakhapatnam	34,940	4.3	35,190	4.1	70,130	4.2
4.	East Godavari	52,910	6.6	23,060	2.7	75,970	4.6
5.	West Godavari	47,366	5.8	36,194	4.2	83,397	5.0
6.	Krishna	40,366	5.0	40,881	4.8	81,247	4.9
7.	Guntur	53,040	6.6	65,235	7.6	118,275	7.1
8.	Prakasam	30,690	3.8	43,230	5.1	73,920	4.5
9.	Nellore	25,033	3.1	26,410	3.1	51,443	3.1
	Rayalaseema Resion					676,964	40.8
10.	Chittor	30,440	3.8	32,290	3.8	62,730	3.8
11.	Cuddapah	19,590	2.4	24,172	2.8	43,762	2.6
12.	Anathapur	45,919	5.7	46,336	5.4	92,255	5.6
13.	Kurnool	54,132	6.7	57,905	6.8	112,037	6.7
	Telangana Region					310,784	18.7
14.	Mahoobnagar	61,260	7.6	63,357	7.4	124,617	7.5
15.	Rangareddy	28,070	3.5	24,090	2.8	52,160	3.1
16.	Hyderabad	11,930	1.5	3,000	0.3	14,930	0.9
17.	Medak	31,820	3.9	33,180	3.9	65,000	3.9
18.	Nizamabad	24,455	3.0	33,699	3.9	58,154	3.5
19.	Adilabad	24,740	3.1	30,513	3.6	55,253	3.3
20.	Karminagar	31,350	3.9	56,213	6.6	87,563	5.3
21.	Warangal	32,790	4.1	42,300	4.9	75,090	4.5
22.	Khammam	33,017	4.1	33,998	4.0	67,015	4.0
23.	Nalgonda	34,150	4.2	40,260	4.7	74,410	4.5
	Total	806,502	100.00	855,438	100.0	1,661,940	40.5

Source: Census of India1991, Series-2 Andhra Pradesh, Part III – B Series, Economic Tables, Directorate of Census Operations, Andhra Pradesh.

Profile of Kurnool District

Administrative Set–up

As per provisional population census figures of 2001, Kurnool district has 10 towns, 54 mandals and 913 villages. This district has a population of about 3.5 million (2001 Census data-Provisional)–(17.8 million males and 17.2 million females) 77.4 per cent of the population is rural. During the decade of 1990s, this district has been facing a trend of urbanisation. Between 1991 and 2001 Kurnool has come down to 9th rank from 12 to 10. If growth of urbanisation is taken as an indicator or development, Kurnool district shows some retrogressive development.

Occupational Distribution

As per 2001 Census, the total labour force in the district is 1,742,677 persons. In the total labour force 22.4 per cent cultivators, 46 per cent agriculture labourers, 3.4 per cent workers in household industry and 28.2 per cent other workers.

Distribution of labour force in Kurnool district is given in Table 5.7.

Nature of Child Labour Occupations-Mandal-wise

Nature of occupations in which children are involved. All the child workers are classified into Mandal wise. These categories are: (1) Stone Quarry (2) Slab Polishing (3) Mineral based Area (4) Lime Kline (5) Quarries and Mines (6) Beedi Making (7) Seed Crossing (8) Agriculture (9) Hotel and Shop Establishments (10) Flower Picking (See the Map).

Literacy Level

During 2001, the literacy rate of the population above six years in Kurnool district stood at 54.4 per cent, where as it is 61.11 per cent for A.P. State. Lowest rate is observed in Kosigi Mandal, which is 27.3 followed by Peddakadabur (29.8) and C. Belgal (34.7). In these Mandals, female literacy is very low compared to the state and district averages. It is 16.2, 16.8 and 20.7 respectively for Kosigi, Peddakadabur and C. Belgal. During 2001, Kosigi and Peddakadabur mandals had about 19 per cent and 20.3 per cent of population as children below six years of age. This indirectly indicates high fertility rate in the overall situation of declining fertility rate in the state.

Table 5.7
Occupational Distribution–Kurnool District

Total/ Rural/ Urban	Persons/ Males/ Females	Total Workers (Main+ Marginal	Cultivators		Agricultural Labourers		Workers in household industry		Other workers	
			Number	%	Number	%	Number	%	Number	%
Total	Persons	1,742,677	390,571	22.4	802,199	46.0	59,211	3.4	490,696	28.2
	Males	1,012,411	255,629	25.2	343,683	33.9	27,460	2.7	385,684	38.2
	Females	730,266	134,942	18.5	458,561	62.8	31,751	4.3	105,012	14.4
Rural	Persons	1,457,455	383,741	26.3	773,117	53.0	36,543	2.5	264,054	18.2
	Males	799,550	250,099	31.3	330,752	41.4	18,503	2.3	200,196	25.0
	Females	657,905	133,642	20.3	442,365	67.2	18,040	2.7	63,858	9.8
Urban	Persons	285,222	6,830	2.4	29,082	10.2	22,668	7.9	226,642	79.05
	Males	212,861	5,530	2.6	12,886	6.1	8,957	4.2	185,488	87.1
	Females	72,361	1,300	1.8	16,196	22.4	13,711	18.9	41,154	56.9

Source: Census of India 2001.

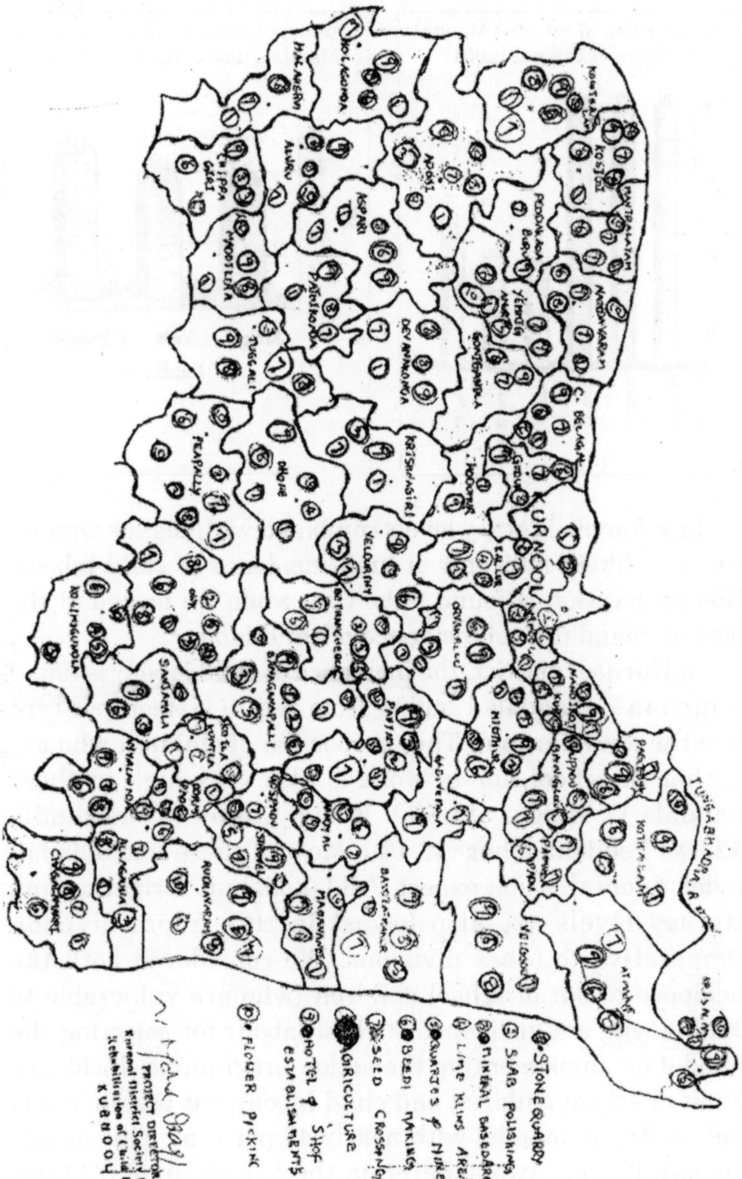
STONE QUARRY
SLAB POLISHING
MINERAL BASED AREA
LIME KILNS AREA
QUARRIES & MINES
BEEDI MAKING
SEED CROSSING
AGRICULTURE
HOTEL & SHOP ESTABLISHMENTS
FLOWER PICKING
PROJECT DIRECTOR
Kurnool District Society for the Rehabilitation of Child Labour
KURNOOL
KURNOOL

Figure 5.1

Literacy rates in selected Mandals of Kurnool District (2001)

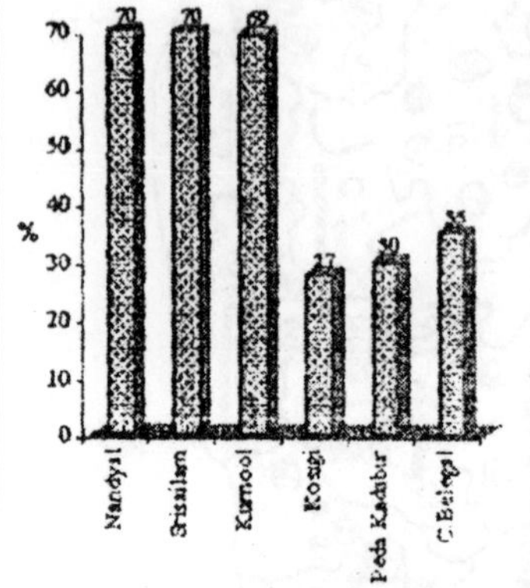

Female Literacy rates in selected Mandals (2001) Kurnool District

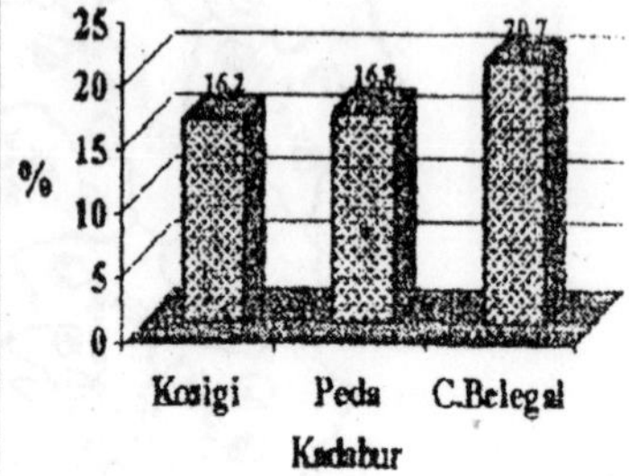

Low female literacy levels combined with higher fertility rate is a likely indicator of high incidence of child labour. This proposition is found to be true when we looked at the data on mandal level incidence of child labour.

In Kurnool district, the incidence of child labour is found to high in 8 mandals ranging from ten to sixteen per cent (See the above graph). The proportion of children who are neither in school nor in work is also very high in these mandals C. Belgal (15.6%), Kosigi (14.5%) Gonegandla (12.9%) Peddakadabur (12.1%). Most of these mandals fall under Adoni division expect Peddakadabur. Irrigation and literacy levels are also lowest in this Adoni division comparative to other divisions. We considered both the incidence of out of school children (who are vulnerable to child labour and incidence of child labour for selecting the mandal for implementing the action programme. Incidence of out of school children and child labour put together it is high in Kosigi mandal with nearly 47 per cent. This means one out of every two children in the age group of 5-14 are either child workers or vulnerable to child work given the backward nature of the region.

Figure 5.2
Incidence of Child Labour in Kurnool District

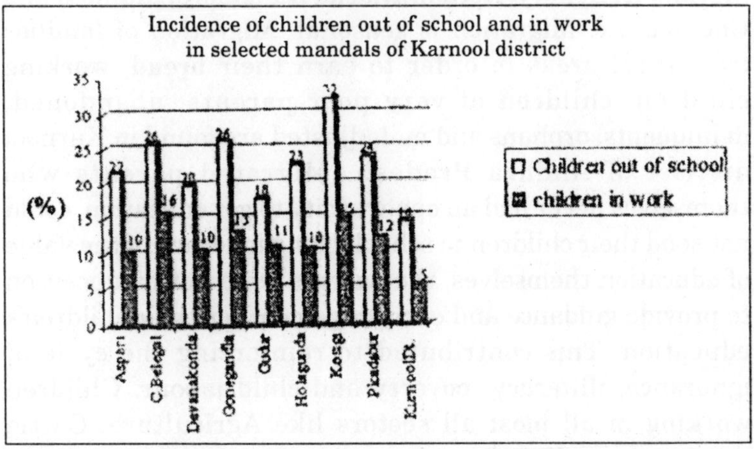

NCLP has done a survey in all the villages during 2000 to see the magnitude of child labour in district. As per this survey there were 10,55,407 children (5,49,356 boys and 50,22,456 girls) in age group of 5-14 in Kurnool district and out of these 55,410 children (26,203 boys and 29,207 girls) are working children. In addition to this there were 1,50,737children (65,162 boys and 85,341 girls) who were out of school. Thus child workers as a proportion to total children in the age group of 5-14 work out to 5.25 per cent. Children who are neither in work nor in school is another 14.3 per cent. While this is the picture that emerges for the whole district there is great variation across mandals in terms of incidence of child labour. Out of 54 mandals, the incidence of child labour is found to be high in 8 mandals ranging from ten to sixteen per cent. The proportion of children who are neither in school nor in work is also very high in these mandals (see the table).

Selection of Kurnool District

Kurnool district had the dubious distinction of having the largest number of child labour, i.e.10,55,407 (NCLP Survey

2000). There is lot of child labour families migrated from Markapur, Bellary, Bethamcharla, Bangalore, Mumbai and Chennai etc. Migration is seasonal. Migration of families from rural areas in order to earn their bread, working children, children of very poor parents, abandoned, delinquents, orphans and maladjusted are found in Kurnool district of Andhra Pradesh. Migrated parents who themselves never had an opportunity to get education, could not send their children to school, being ignorant of the value of education themselves, the parents were not in a position to provide guidance and encouragement for their children's education. This contributed to reinforcing the cycle of ignorance, illiteracy, poverty and child labour. Children working in all most all sectors like Agriculture, Cattle grazing, Lime line, Stone quarries, Shepherds, Livestock, Domestic works, Migrated working in construction, Auto garage, Cycle shops, Petty shops, etc., and they have been deprived of their basic needs and exploited. So, a case study will be undertaken in Kurnool district of Andhra Pradesh in order to examine the miserable conditions of child labour.

Objectives:

1. To identify the socio-economic factors which led to the perpetuation of child labour in Kurnool district.
2. To present the spatial and social dimensions of child labour.
3. To assess the sectoral dimensions.
4. To record the wage pattern of child labour and due to estimate the proportion of their contribution to their family income.
5. To elicit the awareness of different Child Labour Rehabilitation and Regulatory programmes implemented by the State and Central Governments.
6. To suggest the measures which have a regulatory effect on the existence of child labour.

Hypotheses

To give a specific focus to the objective, a few hypotheses have been framed to test the above said objectives by using appropriate statistical tools in the analysis chapter. They are:

1. Level of living conditions of households rise due the earnings of child labour.
2. Low income levels and the parental attitude throw the children into work.
3. Child labours have been denied their basic needs and have been exploited their human rights.
4. Child labours are living under miserable conditions because of their low earnings.

Methodology and Sample Design

The present study intends to survey the socio, economic and occupational patterns of the child labour. For this purpose, both primary and secondary data are to be collected. For secondary data, the Assistant Commissioner of Labour Offices at district level will be visited to get information on the number of child labour. Multi stage random sampling procedure will be used to collect primary data in the more concentrated Child Labour mandals C. Belgal (15.6%), Kosigi (14.5%), Gonegandla (12.9%), Peddakadabur (12.1%) will be selected in Kurnool district of Andhra Pradesh. A total of 300 child labour (samples) will be selected for the study.

Tools of Analysis

For the analysis of data and testing the hypotheses, the following statistical tools are applied:

1. Proportional Analysis under 'Z' Test

To find out whether the contribution of children to the family budget is substantial or not and also to find out whether the families of the working children can maintain themselves without the contribution of child labourers, the Proportional Analysis under 'Z' test is used. The frame work of the analysis is as follows:

$$H_0 = P_1 = P_2$$

$$H_1 = P_1 =/= P_2$$

$$Z = \frac{P_1 - P_2}{\sqrt{\frac{P_1 q_1}{n_1} + \frac{P_2 q_2}{n_2}}}$$

Where,

P_1 = Proportion of adults' contribution

P_2 = Proportion of children's contribution,

q_1 = $1\text{-}P_1$

q_2 = $1\text{-}P_2$

n_1 = number of observations in the first sample,

n_2 = number of observations in the second sample and

$n_1 = n_2 = 300$.

2. *Lorenz Curve and Gini Coefficient*

To test the inequality in the distribution of income before and after the contribution of the child labourers, Lorenz Curve and Gini Coefficient are used. The framework of the analysis of the tests are as follows:

(i) Geometrically, the Gini Coefficient may be defined with respect to Lorenz Curve as:

$$G = 1 \frac{\text{Area between Lorenz Curve and the Diagonal}}{\text{Total area under the Diagonal}}$$

(ii) The algebraic analogue of the geometric definition of the Gini Coefficient is calculated by using the Trapezoidal Rule which is given as:

$$G = 1 \frac{\sum_{k=1}^{n}(P_k - P_{k-1})(Q_k + Q_{k-1})}{10,000}$$

Where,

G = Gini Ratio,

P = Cumulative Percentage of households,

Q = Cumulative Percentage of income, and

n = Number of classes used in the analysis

3. *Sen's Index*

To test the intensity of poverty of the households of the working children before and after the contribution of child labourers, A.K. Sen's Index of Poverty has been applied. The framework of the analysis is as given below:

$$P = H(I + (I–I)\,G)$$

Where,

P = Sen's Index of Poverty,

H = Head Count Ratio,

I = Income – Gap Ratio and

G = Gini coefficient of the income distribution of the individuals below the poverty line.

$$H = \frac{q}{n}$$

Where,

q = number of people below the poverty line,

n = total number of people in the community

I = $\bar{y}/z$

Where,

Z = Poverty cut-off line, that is, income below which poverty begins,

$\bar{y}$ = Average income of the people below the poverty line.

4. Linear Function

To find out whether the employment of children has any impact on household savings before and after their contribution, Linear Function is used. The framework of the analysis is as follows.

$$Y = a + bx$$

Where,

Y = Savings,

a = Constant (intercept),

b = Marginal Propensity to save (slope) and

x = Household income

5. Chi-Square Test

To find out whether there is any association between the employment of children and their earnings in the different occupations at Kurnool, Chi–Square test has been used. The framework of the analysis of Chil–Square test is as follows.

$$x^2 = \Sigma \frac{(0 - E)^2}{E}$$

Where,

O = Observed value and

E = Expected value.

Multiple Linear Regression Model

To analysis the relationship between the magnitude of the child labourers and the size of the family, household income and children's wage earnings, Multiple Linear Regression model is used. The frame work of the analysis takes the following form:

$$Y = a_0 + a_1 X_1 + a_2 X_1 + a_3 X_3 + U$$

Where,

Y = Employment of children in hours of work per annum,

X_1 = Family size,

X_2 = Household income,
X_3 = children's wage earnings,
a_0 = Intercept,
a_1, a_2 and a_3 are partial regression coefficients of the variables X_1, X_2, X_3 respectively and
U = Stochastic disturbance term.

Significance of the Study

It is observed that the rights of the children have been violated and the children are denied of their basic needs or amenities like food, clothing, shelter, education, participation in public life etc. In spite of UN Declaration of Rights of Children in 1989, still the problem is going on increasing instead of decreasing. It is due to economic backwardness or low levels of incomes the poor people, particularly among the rural poor people. We cannot check this problem unless we achieve better levels of income, better standards of living for these groups. Hence, this type of study is necessary.

Relevance of the Study

The vast majority of Child Labours to make living for their families and/or for themselves. Children take up labour work as the adult family members are unemployed and the parental earnings are insufficient. Their parents do not have the capacity to earn enough. The growing cost of living also makes their lives miserable. As a result they have to be involved in some form of labour to feed the family members. Moreover, poor quality schools, poor standards of living, lack of family orientation, low literacy level, backwardness, lack of livelihood resources, crisis in agriculture-loss of crop and debt trap towards studies and desire to earn-all these reasons together slowly pull the children away form education and finally they drop out to become child labourers.

Children are deprived of their right to education; they are deprived of their right to play, leisure an healthy growth; and of free mental, physical, psychological and spiritual growth. Child labour is a violation of a range of child rights. So their rights must be protected and basic needs must be extended to them in order to avoid them child labour and have better social and economic life.

Chapter - 6

CHILD LABOUR: ITS SPATIAL, SOCIAL AND OCCUPATIONAL DIMENTIONS

This chapter is divided into three sections. In the first section an attempt has been made to describe the analysis of the socio-economic characteristics of households of child labourers. In the second section describe working conditions and legal framework. In the third section describes impact of child labour earnings on the level of living households.

Section – I

Analysis of Socio-Economic Characteristics of Households of Child Labourers

The objective of the section is to analysis the distribution of child labourers involved in Kurnool district, based upon the causes, sex, age, educational level, caste, size of the family, type of house, parent's education, dropouts, parent's occupation and income of the child labourers.

Distribution of Child Labour based on the Basic Causes

Poverty is a social curse which makes a section of the society deprived of the basic necessities of life. Poverty line is the cut-off line which demarcates the poor and the non-poor (The studied considers Rs.11,000 per households per annum as the indicator of poverty).

It is generally believed that poverty is the main cause of child labour. There are also other reasons, such as lack of interest in studies, interest in earning, convention and custom of the people of the region and also the influence of the habits of friends, relatives and neighbours of the children, which make them go to work at the school-going age. But poverty is really the most prominent cause of the child labour. This becomes evident from an analysis of the data presented in Table 6.1

Table 6.1
Distribution of Child Labourers based on the Basic Causes, Sex and Age

Sl. No.	*Basic Causes*	*Byos (Years of Age)*			*Girls (Years of Age)*			*Total*
1.	Poverty	5-10	11-13	Total	5-10	11-13	Total	
2.	Not interested in studies	14	13	27 (37.50)	15	113	128 (56.14)	155 (51.67)
3.	Interested in Earning	5	9	14 (19.44)	10	42	52 (22.81)	66 (22.00)
4.	Neighbours are going for work	2	7	9 (12.50)	4	6	10 (4.39)	19 (6.33)
5.	Convention and Custom	3	6	9 (12.50)	13	11	24 (10.52)	33 (11.00)
	Total	28	44	72 (100.00)	47	181	228 (100.00)	300 (100.00)

Source: Computed from Survey Data.

It is seen from Table 6.1 that out of 300 respondents (228 girls and 72 boys) as high as 155 per cent (51.67 per cent) indicated that poverty is the main reason for going to work. Of them, 128 are girls (56.14 per cent of the total number of girls) and 27 are boys (37.5 per cent of the total number of boys). Even at the age of less than 10, girls numbering 5 and boys numbering 14 are forced to work to supplement the family income. This is due to poverty. One hundred and thirteen girls and 13 boys between the age of 11 and 13 years are working because of the same reason.

Another 66 children gave the reason that they are not interested in studies. Of them, 52 are girls (22.81 per cent of the total number of girls) and 14 are boys (19.44 per cent of the total number of boys). Nineteen (6.33 per cent) accepted work because they are interested in earning at the early age. Of them, 10 are girls (4.39 per cent of the total number of girls and nine are boys (12.5 per cent of the total number of boys). Since children in the neighbouring houses and friends are working in the agriculture (cotton field), 27 (9 per cent) children, 14 girls (6.14 per cent of the total number girls) and 13 boys (18.06 per cent of the total number of boys) have taken up job at the school-going age. Convention and custom of the area also influences the children to take up work. About 33 (11 per cent) of the working children expressed that they come to Agricultural field to stick to the custom and convention of working at early age, so as to add to the family income.

On the basis of these findings, it can be inferred that though child labour is the result of various causes, poverty is the main cause for the prevalence of child labour. In this study, 155 (51.67 per cent) have directly informed to me. My parents are forced to work, because of insufficient income of the family and to supplement the family income. The custom and convention of the lowest classes is another indirect cause for sending them to work since their parents' income is low and it becomes a custom and convention among them to work at an early age to earn for the family.

It can be seen from Table 6.2 that 84 (28 per cent)child labourers have never been to school. A higher proportion of girls than boys are illiterate, the percentage being 28.95 of the total number of girls and 25 of the total number of boys.

Among boys 18 (25 per cent) are illiterate, 42 (58.33 per cent) attended the primary school and 12 (16.67 per cent) attended middle school. Among girls 66 (28.95 per cent) are illiterate, 126 (55.26 per cent) attended primary classes and

36 (15.79 per cent) attended the middle school level. In short, a majority (56 per cent) of the working children have been to school and dropped out before they have completed the fifth year of schooling. Since the study is of child laboures of below 14 years of age, there is no possibility for them to attend schools after eighth year of schooling.

Table 6.2
Distribution of Child Labourers based on the Educational level and Sex

Sl. No.	*Educational Level*	*Boys*	*%*	*Girls*	*%*	*Total*	*%*
1.	Illiterate	18	25	66	28.95	84	28
2.	Primary	42	58.33	126	55.26	168	56
3.	Middle	12	16.67	36	15.79	48	16
	Total	72	100	228	100	300	100

Source: Computed from Survey Data.

From the table we understand that both male and female children have not been afforded educational opportunities which are due to them. The skill, efficiency and the knowledge of the future citizens of India are checked due to their employment in these industrial units.

Distribution of Child Labourers based on the Education and Caste

Table 6.3 shows the distribution of child laborers based on the education and caste.

It appears from Table 6.3 that 11 (3.67 per cent) child labourers belong to the backward class are illiterate. Scheduled caste 31 (10.33 per cent) are illiterate, where it is 42 (14 per cent) among the other caste. Further, data analysis shows that the total illiteracy percentage among all the castes of the working children is 28. It means literacy percentage is 72. Thirty-three children (11 per cent) of the child workers belonging to the backward class have primary school education, among the scheduled cast, it is 72 (24 per cent) and among the other caste, it is 63 (21 per cent). Nineteen (6.33 per cent) child labourers belong to the backward classes have middle school education among the most scheduled class, it is five (1.67 per cent) and other caste, it is 24 (8 per cent) only. These findings show that the scheduled and other castes though economically not well off in comparison to the backward caste, are socially more aware of the value of education.

Table 6.3
Distiribution of Child Laborers based on the Education and Caste

Sl. No.	*Education*	*Community*							
		BC	*%*	*SC*	*%*	*Others*	*%*	*Total*	*%*
1.	Illiterate	11	3.67	31	10.33	42	14	84	28
2.	Primary	33	11	72	24	63	21	168	56
3.	Middle	19	6.33	5	1.67	24	8	48	16
	Total	63	21	108	36	129	43	300	100

Source: Computed from survey Data.

Distribution Child Labourers based on the size of the Family and Caste

Large families with a comparatively low income cannot have happiness in their lives. As a result, they cannot give good shelter to their children. If a family is limited and well planned, there will be no question of sending children to work. In view of these facts, information has been gathered from 300 respondent child labourers and presented in Table 6.4.

It is shown in Table 6.4 that the common size of the family is 4 to 6 in backward as well as in the scheduled and other castes. The table further shows that 188 (62.67 per cent) families have 4 to 6 members and families with 7 to 10 are 71 (23.67 per cent) only families with more than 10 members are insignificant. There are only 28 (9.33 per cent) families with three or less members.

Table 6.4
Distribution of Child Laobures based on the size of the Family and Caste

Sl. No.	*Caste*	*No. of Family Members* 1-3	4-6	7-10	Above 10	Total
1.	BC	6	37	17	3	63
		(2.00)	(12.34)	(5.67)	(1.00)	(21.00)
2.	SC	12	61	32	3	108
		(4.00)	(20.33)	(10.67)	(1.00)	(36.00)
3.	Others	10	90	22	7	129
		(3.33)	(30.00)	(7.33)	(2.33)	(43.00)
	Total	28	188	71	13	300
		(9.33)	(62.67)	(23.67)	(4.33)	(100.00)

Source: Computed from Survey Data.

Distribution of Child Laborers based on the type of House and Caste

The type of house and caste distribution of child labourers are presented in Table 6.5.

Table 6.5
Distribution of Child Labourers based on the type of House and Caste

Sl. No.	*Type of House*	*Community* BC	%	SC	%	Others	%	Total	%
1.	Thatched	5	1.67	63	21	71	23.67	139	46.34
2.	Tiled	21	7	27	9	37	12.33	85	28.33
3.	Terraced	37	12.33	18	6	21	7	76	25.33
	Total	63	21	108	36	129	43	300	100

Source: Computed from Survey Data.

The data presented in Table 6.5 show that 139 (46.34 per cent) child workers live in thatched houses, 85 (28.33 per cent) in tiled houses and 76 (25.33 per cent) in terraced houses. Out of 139 respondents living in thatched houses five (1.67 per cent) belong to backward caste 63 (21 per cent) to scheduled caste and 71 (23-67 per cent) to other caste. These data confirm that it is the poor that join the labour force during their child hood since housing is an indication of poverty.

Distribution of Child Labourers based on the Education and Parents and the Parents' Education

Table 6.6 clearly illustrates the distribution of child labourers based on the education and the parents' education.

Table 6.6
Distribution of Child Labourers based on the Education and the Parents' Education

S1 No.	*Level of Education*	*Father*	*%*	*Mother*	*%*	*Child Labourers*	*%*
1.	Illiterate	139	48.26	116	39.86	84	28
2.	Primary	136	47.22	149	51.20	168	56
3.	Middle	13	4.52	26	8.94	48	16
	Total	288	100	291	100	300	100

Source: Computed from Survey Data.
Note: Twelve children have no father, therefore, total number of fathers shown is 288 only and nine children have no mothers, therefore, total number of mothers shown is 291 only.

It is evident from Table 6.6 that 139 (48.26 Per cent) fathers and 116 (39.86 per cent) mothers are illiterate, whereas only 84 (28 per cent) child labourers are found to have been deprived of education. Further, the table reveals that 136 (47.22 per cent). 149 (51.20 per cent) mothers and 168 (56 per cent) child labourers have attended primary schools. Thirteen (14.52 per cent) fathers, 26 (8.94 per cent) mothers and 48 (16 per cent) child labourers have attended middle schools. This analysis reveals that even the educated parents (149 fathers and 175 mothers) send their children to work at an early age. This means that poverty and ignorance force the parents to send their children to work place rather than to school.

Distirubution of Dropouts of Child Labourers based on the Level of Education

Since the child labourers come almost from poor families. They cannot continue their education even up the middle school level. Hence, most of them leave the schools even during the period of the primary classes. Table 6.7 shows the distribution of dropouts of child laborers based on the years of schooling and sex.

Table 6.7
Distribution of Drop outs of Child Labourers based on the Level of Education

Sl. No.	*Year of Schooling*	*Boys*	*%*	*Girls*	*%*	*Total Children*	*%*
1.	I Standard	6	8.33	21	9.21	27	9
2.	II Standard	4	5.56	25	10.96	29	9.67
3.	III Standard	8	11.12	28	12.28	36	12
4.	IV Standard	9	12.50	21	9.21	30	10
5.	V Standard	15	20.83	31	13.60	46	15.33
6.	VI Standard	6	8.33	12	5.26	18	6
7.	VII Standard	4	5.56	15	6.58	19	6.33
8.	VIII Standard	2	2.77	9	3.95	11	3.67
9.	Illiterate	18	25	66	28.95	84	28
	Total	72	100	228	100	300	100

Source: Computed from Survey Data.

It appears from Table 6.7 that out of 300 child labourers covered by the study, 84 (28 per cent) are illiterate which includes 18 boys (25 per cent of the total number of boys) and 66 girls (28.95 per cent of the total number of girls). Six boys (8.33 Per cent) and 21 girls (9.21 per cent) have dropped out after the first year of schooling. In aggregate 29 (9.67 per cent) working children covered by the study have dropped out after the second year of schooling. Among the 29 drop outs at this levels, four of them are boys (5.56 per cent of the total number of boys) and the rest are girls (10.96 per cent of the total number of girls). Out of 300 samples, 36 (12 per cent) working children have dropped out after the third year of schooling. This covers eight boys (11.12 per cent of the total number of boys) and 28 girls (12.28 per cent of the total number of girls). After the fourth year of schooling, there are 30 (10 per cent) dropouts in the sample; nine of them are boys (12.50 per cent of the total number of boys) and 21 are girls (9.21 per cent of the total number of girls). Forty-six (15.33 per cent) working children left the school after the fifth year of schooling. Of this, 15 are boys (20. 83 per cent of the total number of boys) and 31 are girls (13.60 per cent of the total number of girls).

There are 18 (6 per cent) dropouts after sixth year of schooling. Of this, six are boys (8.33 per cent of the total number of boys) and 12 are girls (5.26 per cent of the total number of girls). Out of the 300 child labourers covered by this study, 19 (6.33 per cent) have dropped out after seventh year of schooling; among them four are boys (5.56 per cent of the total number of boys) and 15 are girls (6.58 per cent of the total number of girls). The 11 drop-outs (3.67 per cent) after the eighth year of schooling consist of two boys (2.77 per cent of the total number of boys) and nine girls (3.95 per cent of the total number of girls).

Distribution of Child Labourers based on the Parent's Occupation and Type of Work

Some observations can also made from the occupational status of the parents of the working children. For this purpose, the children working in the match industry have been classified based on the occupations of both fathers and mothers.

Table 6.8 highlights the fact that 115 (38.34 per cent) fathers are agricultural labourers, 52 (17.33 per cent) fathers have agriculture as their occupation, 37 (12.33 per cent) are involved in construction work, 33 (11 per cent) stone quarrying work and 25 (8.33 per cent) in other occupations, 26 (8.67 per cent) fathers are non-workers, 12 (4 per cent) children have no children.

Distribution of Child Labourers based on the Father's Occupation

In Table 6.8, the occupations of fathers' vis-a-vis those of the child labourers have been presented.

Table 6.8
Distribution of Child Labourers Based on the Fathers' Occupation and Type of Work

Sl. No.	*Fathers' Occupation Labour*	*Category of Work of the Child Labourers*					
		Agricul. Labour	*Constru. Quarry*	*Stone Klines*	*Lime Grazing*	*Cattle*	*Total*
1.	Agricultural Labour	92	16	3	1	3	115 (38.34)
2.	Cultivation	19	15	16	1	1	52 (17.33)
3.	Stone Quarrying	16	17	2	2	—	37 (12.33)
4.	Construction Labour	18	10	2	3	—	33 (11.00)
5.	Other Occupation	7	12	5	1	—	25 (8.33)
6.	Non-Workers	15	8	2	1	—	26 (8.67)
7.	Fatherless	5	3	3	—	1	12 (4.00)
	Total	172	81	33	9	5	300

Source: Computed from Survey Data.

From this one can easily conclude that uneducated fathers who are employed in Agriculture Labour, Cultivation, Construction Labour, Other occupations their send their children for work in the same occupations. Thus, it concludes that the occupation of the fathers as well as their educational level has much influence on the children's education and the choice of present work.

Distribution of Child Labourers based on the Mother's Occupation and Type of Work

Table 6.9 illustrates the distribution of child labourers based on the mothers' occupations.

Table 6.9
Distribution of Child Labourers based on the Mothers' Occupation and Type of Work

Sl. No.	*Mothers' Occupation*	*Category of Work of the Child Labourers*					
		Agricul. Labour	*Constru. Labour*	*Stone Quarry*	*Lime Kline's*	*Cattle Grazing*	*Total*
1.	Agricultural Labour	77	31	10	2	1	121 (40.33)
2.	Lime Kline	43	25	9	1	—	78 (26.00)
3.	Stone Quarrying	36	13	6	1	1	57 (19.00)
4.	Construction Labour	7	2	5	3	1	18 (6.00)
5.	Other Occupation	4	8	3	2	—	17 (5.67)
6.	Non-Workers	5	2	—	—	2	9 (3.00)
	Total	172	81	33	9	5	300 (100)

Source: Computed from Survey Data.

From Table 6.9 one can find that 121 (40.33 per cent) children come from houses where the mothers are working in Agriculture Labourers, 78 (26 per cent) Lime Kline, 57 (19 per cent) Stone quarrying, 18 (6 per cent) Construction Labour 17 (5.67 per cent), mother of child labourers are Other Occupations, 9 (3.00) Non-Workers.

It can also be observed from the table that there is a significant relationship between mothers' occupations and the children's occupations. Thus, the mother's occupation influences the type of the child's work. It is because of the fact when mothers are going for work, they send their children for work also; especially when the mothers are employed in the Agriculture field, they used to take other children with them at an early age. When they are sitting near the mothers, they easily learn the art of the mother's occupation and thus take to the same type of work. Thus, the parents' occupation has much in deciding the children's occupations.

Distribution of Child Labourers based on the Annual Income of the Parents

The annual income of the parents of child labourers has been divided into different groups as presented in Table 6.10. The annual Income of the parent's includes the income from agricultural sources.

Table 6.10
Distribution of Child Labourers based on the Annual Income of the Parents

Sl. No.	*Income Group*	*Number of the child labourers*	*Percentage*
1.	Up to 5,000	135	45.00
2.	5,001 to 7,000	101	33.67
3.	7,001 to 10,000	35.	11.67
4.	Above 10,000	29	9.66
	Total	300	100

Source: Computed from Survey Data.

It is obvious from Table 6.10 that 135 (45 per cent) parents have annual income of less than Rs. 5,000 while 101 (33.67 per cent), 35 (11.67 per cent) and 29 (9.66 per cent) parents have annual income between Rs. 5001 and Rs. 7,000, Rs. 7,001 and Rs. 10,000 and above Rs. 10,000 respectively. This indicates that due to the low income of the family, children are deprived of the educational and other facilities which are essential for the proper growth and development.

Since the annual income of the families is low, the children are sent to workplaces as labourers. The table clearly indicates that higher the income of the family, the lower the number of children employed (See the Table 6.10). Hence, the argument that to abolish child labour, the annual income of the families is to be increased, holds good to a great extent.

Distribution of Child Laborers based on the Education and their Annual Income

It is considered that educated parents have more knowledge, sense of responsibility and understanding than uneducated parents. Therefore, the parents have to be impressed about the need of education for their wards. Further, the parents should be employed so as to enable them to get adequate wages for the sustenance of their families and for spending towards the education of their children. The distribution of child labourers based on the education and their annual income is presented in Table 6.11.

Table 6.11
Distribution Child Labourers based on the Education and their Annual Income

Sl. No.	*Educational Level*	*Annual Income (in Rupees)*				
		Up to 3,000	*3001 to 4,000*	*4,001 to 5,000*	*Above 5,000*	*Total*
1.	Illiterate	19 (6.33)	36 (12.00)	20 (6.67)	9 (3.00)	84 (28.00)
2.	Primary	38 (12.67)	50 (16.67)	17 (5.66)	63 (21.00)	168 (56.00)
3.	Middle	9 (3.00)	4 (1.33)	13 (4.33)	22 (7.34)	48 (16.00)
	Total	66 (22.00)	90 (30.00)	50 (16.66)	94 (31.34)	300 (100)

Source: Computed from Survey Data.

It is evident from Table 6.11 that the educated child labourers earned more than illiterate ones. Out of 84 (28 per cent) illiterate child labourers, 19 (6.33 per cent) earn less than Rs. 3,000, 36 (12 per cent) earn between Rs. 3,001 and Rs. 4,000, 20 (6.67 per cent) between Rs. 4,001 and 5,000, whereas nine (3 per cent) earn above Rs. 5,000.

Again out of 168 (56 per cent) respondents who attended the primary school, 38 (12.67 per cent) earn less than Rs. 3,000, 50 (16.67 per cent) between Rs. 3,001 and Rs. 4,000, 17 (5.66 per cent) between Rs. 4,001 and Rs. 5,000 and 63 (21 per cent) above Rs. 5,000. Out of 48 (16 per cent) who attended the middle school, nine (3 per cent) earn less than Rs. 3,000, four (1.33 per cent) earn between Rs. 3,001 and Rs. 4,000, 13 (4.33 per cent) between Rs. 4,001 and Rs. 5,000 and 22 (7.34 per cent) above Rs. 5,000.

Recapitulation

The analysis of the socio-economic characteristics of households of child labourers household reveals important findings of some causes for child labour based on the age, sex, educational level, caste, size of the family, type of house, parents' education, dropouts, parent's occupation and income, and income of the child labourers. Out of 300 child labourers covered by this study, 72 (24 per cent) are boys and 228 (76 per cent) are girls. This implies that female child labourers more in number that male child labourers in the study area. Further, 155 (51.67 per cent) indicated that poverty is the main reason for going to work.

Regarding educational levels of the child labourers, it is observed that 28 per cent are illiterate and the remaining educated child labourers have not crossed the middle school level. About 56 per cent of the selected child labourers have completed primary level education.

The caste-wise distribution of child labour reveals that majority of them are from the other castes which constitute a majority of the population in the study area. An interesting finding is the relationship between the number of child labourers and the size of their families. The large size families are contributing a higher number of child labourers from the selected households.

The analysis of dropouts and educational level of child laborers reveals that a large number (46 per cent) of the child labourers have dropped out of school after completion of the fifth standard, the primary level of schooling.

The distribution of the child labourers based on the parent's occupation reveals the parent's occupation has much influence in deciding the children's occupation. Regarding the annual income of the parents of child labourers, it is observed that due to the low income of the family, children are sent to work places as labourers. Further, the distribution of child labourers according to the size of their annual income exhibits that a large proportion (31.34 per cent) is form the income group above Rs. 5,000.

Section – II

Working Conditions and Legal Framework

This examines the employment of child labours in different occupations. Further, it describes the working conditions of child labourers.

The main purpose of this section is to assess from our sample size of 300 child workers interviewed, the structure and pattern of employment of children in the different occupations of high concentrated child labour mandals, namely Kosigi, Peddakadabur, C. Belagl, and Gonegandala in Kurnool District.

Employment Pattern

Agricultural Labourers

Children working as agricultural labourers are engaged in fields where cotton, sunflower and groundnut are produced. Majority of the children are involved in cotton fields.

In the recent past, since 1990s, some outsiders started leasing in land from this people to cultivate a new variety of cotton seeds. They prefer only child workers. They arrive a little early before cultivation starts and conduct a 'survey' on availability of children to work in the cotton field. Child employment is justified with the superstition (made possible due to illiteracy as well) that those who have attained puberty should not enter the cotton field. After identifying the potential child workers, these 'Landlords' also pay advance money to the parents before employing children. This has an element of bondage.

In some, cases the middle men or contractors who make a living from this entire business, they pay small amounts to parents of these children and get many times more, for providing their services, from the field owners.

Children are employed for manually pollinating the cotton flowers and also for crushing the male buds after pollination. Each child gets about Rs. 20 per day for about ten hours of work. In a week, they earn about Rs. 120 to Rs.140. The 'pocket money' that children got acted as an additional incentive for the children to go for work instead of education.

It is calculated that ten children are required full time for cultivating cottonseed in one acre. The most important thing about this cottonseed cultivation is that 90 per cent of the labour force required is from children below the age of 11 to 13 years. Thus the incidence of child labour has been increasing in the cotton field cultivation.

Cultivation of cotton-seed is done in large quantities. A myth that only children who have not attained puberty should be involved in cross-pollination and weeding activities is prevalent. The exposure to harmful effects of pesticides increases vulnerability of children to various diseases. The burden of domestic work and seasonal work for the girl child causes them to fail/dropout of school.

Construction Labour

Lack of adequate resource, assetlessness and employment opportunities force them to migrate. Mohammed Isque, Project Director, NCLP, Kurnool says, "The landless agricultural workers and the marginal farmers affected the most in a drought situation. While the elders migrate out of sheer poverty and debt, they drag along hapless school-going children, forcing them to dropout from education". While parents keep them busy in the construction works, the children are involved in manual transporting, tending and conditioning wall under the sun. However, the greatest loss these children suffer is their access to basic education and a secure, carefree childhood. With their parents becoming regular migrants and staying away from the village for 4-6 months a year, the children lose out on primary education. Continuous absence from school often lead to their names being struck off from the register and poverty prevents their re-enrolment. As a result, they are force into wage labour even when they are back in the villages.

Stone Quarrying

In stone quarrying work starts early in the morning. In summer, it starts 5.30 a.m and ends by 11.30 a.m. In the winter season 7.30 a.m to 1 p.m. Children are sincere and the job without any protest. There wages are low compared to those of the adults. The average daily income of many such facilities is less than Rs.50 to Rs.70. In most cases children also accompany their parents. One they move out of work along with their families there ends their children's education. A section of quarrying involves the pitching of stones. Most children do not wear any masks.

Child labour in mining and quarrying it finds that mining is one of the three most dangerous occupations to work in along with agriculture and construction. Blasting is common in Quarrying and Mining. Generally, blasting is done after normal working hours when the labourers have left. Sometimes, barefooted children have unknowingly stepped on these unexploded detonators. In spite of all these hazards, the children are sincere and do their work without any protest.

Quarry workers have shown a high incidence of tuberculosis, silicosis, chronic bronchitis and other respiratory problems (The Times of India, Mumbai, Saturday, July 23, 1994).

Lime Kline's and Construction Labour

An economic condition of the households is an important factor to determine the child labour. Most of the Lime Kline's labour households do not have land and other source of income. Consequently, their livelihood depends mainly on the income from Lime Kline's. In majority of the house holds borrowed to maintain their livelihood. Under this situation children drop out schools and engaged in Lime Kline's work. The lime Kline's work shut down during the monsoon. During the rainy season children working as agricultural labourers are engaged in field where ground nut, cotton and sunflower are produced.

Some Case Studies of Working Children

Case Study: 1

One of my interviews is with Subramanyam a 12 years old child labour working in the Lime Klines for the past 5 years, his daily activity starts from morning 70' clock and ends at 6 p.m. His mother is physically handicapped. His father was died last five years back. At that time I was begging in platform in Guntakal Railway Station few months, afterwards he was joined in Lime Kline's, the boy trembling fingers and tears in his eyes. The voice shaky, the words slurred a little. My eyes and ache every day after I return from home. Often I feel suffocated and vomit due to smell of Lime Kline's fume.

Case Study: 2

I asked some children how they heard that work was available in cotton filed. Rahim (10 years) said: "Contractors come to the villages and say they want children so we know in (cotton field) there is work. Often the contractors don't want to give the work adults. We are young, we can work in the cotton fields. Because cotton bushes are short, the short height of children makes them ideal for wok in cotton fields. One more reason we did not trouble to landlords."

Case Study: 3

Narasaiah (13) studied up to class in his native village (V Vandagallu). He discontinued his study as he considered he was not good in study and secondly, they left their native villages for Peddakadabur it was his father's wish to join the work force and earn something since by talking education he cannot do anything. Whereas if he learn a skill he can earn his livelihood. It is also observed that some left their schools as they were not good students or had failed the examinations. Actually, the fact is that infrastructure facilities in schools are limited and secondly, parents do have any time to guide their children. So, children dropout and join the workforce.

Distribution of Working Childrens based on the Type of Work, Age and Sex

Table 6.12 gives the distribution of the interviewed child labourers on the basis of the type of work performed by them their age and sex.

It can be observed, children of both sexes are involved, though in different proportions. In aggregate 228 (76 per cent) girls and 72 (24 per cent) boys are engaged in different occupations covered by this study. The ratio between girls and boys is 3.17:1 which indicates that girls are preferred to boys by the employers, since they are easily controllable. Moreover, in most of the families, boys are persuaded by their parents to attend school and girls' education is not considered as important as the education of the boys. This shows the discrimination against girls by their own parents. This trend further brings to light the discrimination followed in the case of girls, for, the girls are taken for granted and they are denied of the educational and other opportunities due to all children.

In Agriculture Labour 48 (66.67 per cent) boys and (54.39 per cent) girls are engaged. In the construction work, eight (11.11 per cent) boys and 73 (32.01 per cent) girls are engaged. In aggregate, Agricultural attracted more children whose number is 172. The percentage works out 57.33. The reason is that children's are getting other incentives in the agricultural work.

Table 6.12
Distribution of Child Laborers based on the Type of Work, Age and Sex

Sl. No.	*Category of Work*	*Sex*						
		Boys (Years of age)			*Girls (Years of age)*			*Total*
		5 to 10	*11 to 13*	*Total*	*5 to 10*	*11 to 13*	*Total*	
1.	Agriculture Labour	21	27	48 (66.67)	31	93	124 (56.39)	172 (57.33)
2.	Construction Labour	7	1	8 (11.11)	15	58	73 (32.01)	81 (27.00)
3.	Stone Quarrying	—	2	2 (2.78)	1	30	31 (13.60)	33 (11.00)
4.	Lime Kline	—	9	9 (12.50)	—	—	—	9 (3.00)
5.	Cattle Grazing	—	5	5 (6.94)	—	—	—	
	Total	28	44	72 (100.00)	47	181	228 (100.00)	300 (100.00)

Source: Computed from Survey Data.

Of the 300 children interviewed, 172 are engaged in Agricultural work, 81 in Construction work, 33 in Stone quarrying nine in Lime Kline and five are Cattle grazing. The data collected regarding the hours of work of child labourers during the present surveys is presented in Table 6.13.

Table 6.13 shows that 135 (45 per cent) child labourers have revealed that they worked for nine to eleven hours per day, 108 (36 per cent) for six to eight hours, 30 (10 per cent) for more than 11 hours while 27 (9 per cent) worked for five hours or less. This is mainly due to the fact that the child labourers are paid according to their output. They are found working from the early hours of morning till late in the evening along with their parents.

Table 6.13
Distribution of Child Labourers Based on the Daily Hours of Work

Sl. No.	*Working Hours*	*Number of child Labourers*	*Percentage*
1.	Up to 5	27	9
2.	6 to 8	108	36
3.	9 to 11	135	45
4.	Above 11	30	10
	Total	300	100

Source: Computed from Survey Data.

Distribution of Child Labourers based on the Effect of Work on their Health

As for as the impact of work on the health of the child labour is concerned, the information from child labourers is collected and presented in Table 6.14.

Table 6.14
Distribution of Child Labourers based on the Effect of Work on their Health

Sl. No.	*Nature of Effect of Work*	*Number of child Labourers*	*Percentage*
1.	Back pain	97	32.33
2.	Body pain	43	14.33
3.	High fever (Many times)	41	13.67
4.	Sore eye	37	12.33
5.	Giddiness	29	9.67
6.	Chest pain	26	8.67
7.	Asthma	18	6.00
8.	Not Responded	9	3.00
	Total	300	100.00

Source: Computed from Survey Data.

It appears from Table 6.14 that 97 cases (32.33 per cent) of Back pain found among children. Similarly, body pain, Sore eye, high fever, giddiness, chest pain, asthma reported by 43, 41, 37, 29, 26, 18, and 9 respectively. The most common diseases were back pain, body pain, high fever, giddiness, headache, chest pain, asthma etc.

Legal Framework

The Role of International Labour Organisation (ILO)

The International Labour Organisation has played a significant role in combating child labour since its first conference held in 1919. It has passed Conventions and Recommendations regulating the minimum age of admission of children into various forms of employment.

Convention No.138 passed by the ILO in 1973 keeping 15 years as the minimum age for employment was ratified by its Member States. The International Programme on Elimination of Child Labour (IPEC) is a major programme of ILO in combating the evil of child labour. The IPEC programme is global and Technical Advisory Services to all ILO Member States are provided on their request by it initially Brazil, India, Indonesia, Kenya, Thailand and Turkey were selected as priority countries for implementation of IPEC. The programme is being extended in four more countries: Bangladesh, Pakistan, the Philippines and Tanzania.

It is believed that a joint battle by government, workers, employers, NGOs, educators, parents and children against child labour is necessary in particular, for action against the worst abuses of child labour, hazardous work, bonded child labour, forced child labour, the employment of children who are less than 12 or 13 years old, girls and street children.

From 1919 until today, the unique feature of the ILO has been its tripartite structure which brings together governments, employers and workers at all levels of decision making. Its basic principles are: (a) labour is not a commodity; (b) freedom of expression and association are essential for sustained progress; and (c) all human beings have the right to pursue their material and spiritual development in conditions of freedom, dignity, economic security and equal opportunity.

International Programme for Elimination of Child Labour (IPEC)

This is an Action Programme which has been established by the ILO, commencing work in 1990. The ILO entered into an agreement with the Government of Germany in December 1991 for implementing the programme over a period of five years with an assistance of DM 50 million. In 1992, Belgium also became a donor in the programme. India was one of the first countries to join the programme which is now under implementation in 10 countries. The long term objective of IPEC is to contribute to effective abolition of child labour. In the two financial years 1992-93 and 1994-95, allocation for India given under IPEC is US $ 3.65 million. Altogether 89 projects with an outlay of Rs. 85 million have been approved and are under different stages of implementation. An amount of Rs. 73 million has been spent. The total number of children covered by these 89 projects is about 55,000. Another, 12 projects with an outlay of Rs. 4.8 million to cover about 24,000 children are pending approval.

Legislative Provisions for Child Labour

Various enactments introduced from time to time to protect the child labour have child labour have been discussed in the following pages:

1. The Employment of Children Act, 1938

The legislation as to child labour, regulating the employment of children, namely, Employment of Children Act was enacted in 1938. This Act prohibits the employment of children, in certain occupations, who are below the age of 15 years. It also lyses down the working hours and restrictions on employment of children in the job as apprentice in workshops, who have not completed the age of 14 years. This enactment provides machinery to watch the enforcement of the Act, and coercive methods of its implementation by providing punishment for the contravention.

2. *Factories Act, 1948*

The Act regulates employment of children in certain occupations connected with transport of passengers, goods or mail by railways and with the handling of goods within the limits of any port. The Act prohibits employment of children below 15 years of age in the above occupations.

The Act forbids employment of children below the age of 14 in workshops connected with (i) Bidi-making (ii) Cement manufacture (iii) Carpet-weaving (iv) Cloth-printing (v) Dyeing and weaving (vi) Manufacture of matches (vii) Explosives and fireworks (viii) Tanning and wool-cleaning. The Act was extended subsequently to a few more industries.

The railway administration and port authorities are required to maintain registers showing names and dates of birth of children below 17 years employed by them and fix their periods of work, intervals of rest, nature of work, etc. in pursuance of the Act, the Government of India has framed the Employment of Children (Railways) Rules, 1955 and the Employment of Children (Major Ports) Rules, 1955. These rules relate to the grant of rest intervals, maintenance of registers for children below 15-17 years of age, etc. For ports and railways, the administrative authority, as per the Act, is the Chief Labour Commissioner (Central), whereas in the States, it is either Chief Inspector of Factories or the Labour Commissioner.

3. *Minimum Wages Act, 1948*

This Act makes provision for fixation of minimum rates of wages in certain employment which have been specified by appropriate government in the scheduled of the Act. The Act maintains some expressions of adult, adolescent and child as in case of Factories Act, 1948. The Act does not make any specific provisions except that it says that different minimum rates of wages may be fixed for adults adolescent and children (Section 3). Rule 24 of the Minimum Wages (Central) Rules, 1950 provides that in the case of a child the number of hours in a normal working day shall be 4½. Thus, it can be concluded that the Minimum Wages Act provides for a work day of 4½ hours and differential rates of minimum for child workers.

4. *The Plantation Labour Act, 1951*

This Act covers all tea, coffee, rubber, cinchona and cardamom plantations in an area of 10.117 hectare or more and in which 30 or more persons are employed. Employment of children below the age of 12 is prohibited under this Act. No child who has not completed 12 of age and no adolescent person between the age of 15-18 can be allowed to work in any plantation (Section 26) unless he is certified fit to work by a duly appointed certifying surgeon and unless he carries a token to this effect while at work. Certificate given is valid only for one year. For children (below 15 years of age) and adolescents (15-18 years of age), the Act prescribes a maximum of 40 hours of work a week.

5. *The Mines Act, 1952*

No child below the age of 15 can be employed in mines. Even an adolescent cannot be employed below ground unless he has completed 16 years and should be certified fir to work as an adult by a certifying surgeon and carries a token to that effect while at work. An adolescent not certified fir to work as an adult cannot be employed or permitted to employ above ground in a mine for more than four and half hours on any day and between 6 p.m and 6 a.m.

6. *Merchant Shipping Act, 1958*

The act applies to ships registered in India. Employment of children below the age of 15 is prohibited under the Act. Similarly, employment of young persons below 18 years of age as trimmers and stokers is also generally prohibited. Such persons, if employed, are required, to produce a certificate of fitness from a prescribed authority. Further, the Act empowers the Government to make necessary rules regarding employment of young persons as and when the occasion demands.

7. *The Motor Transport Workers Act, 1961*

The Act prohibits the employment of children who have not completed years of age in any capacity in motor transport undertaking. Adolescents are not allowed to work as transport workers unless a certificate of fitness is given by a certifying surgeon.

8. *The Atomic Energy Act, 1962*

The quite new field of development of industries is atomic energy. But atomic energy has not yet been tamed so as to be handled by an ordinary man. Therefore, it has no chances of employment of child labour.

From looking into various fields of employment, it will be revealed that child labour is employed because it being unskilled labour is cheaper. It can be exploited because it is available only because of the dire need of money on account or poverty. It is also on account of exploitation of the wards by the guardians also. In private organisations like orphanages, the children are exploited by the organisers. Legislations like 'The Children's Act 1960' are enacted so that the management of such institutions cannot exploit the children their custody.

The Central Government has made the Radiation Protection Rules 1971 under section 30 of the Act. Rule 5 of these rules prohibits the employment of person below the age of 18 years as radiation workers, except with the prior permission in writing of the competent authority, that is to sayan officer or an authority, are appointed in this behalf by the Central Government as notification under those rules.

The Central as well as the State Government have taken caution as much as possible by the above legislations, but until there is restriction on the parents, the problem of child labour will not extinguish.

9. *The Bidi and Cigar Workers (Conditions of Employment) Act, 1966*

The Act prohibits employment of children below the age of 14 in any industrial premises. Employment of young persons between 14-18 years of age is prohibited between 7 p.m and 6 a.m.

10. *Child Labour (Prohibition and Regulation) Act, 1986*

The Child Labour Prohibition and Regulation Act, 1986 is an outcome of various recommendations made by a series of committees such as National Commission on Labour, 1969, Gurupadaswamy and Sanat Mehta.

The Child Labour (Prohibition & Regulation) Bill was introduced by the government in the two Houses of Parliament. The Provision regarding unions of child labour was dropped and also excluded provision for child workers to go and report to the inspectors. The provision for imposition of access on the employers was also done away with; the Bill in its true form intended to–

1. Basic employment of children i.e. those who have not completed their 14th year in specified occupations and process.

2. Lay down a procedure to decide modifications to the schedule of banned occupations and/or processes.
3. Regulate the condition of work of children in employment they are not prohibited from working.
4. Lay down enhanced formalities for employment of children in violation of the provisions of the Act and other Acts which forbid the employment of children.
5. To obtain uniformity in the definition of child in the related laws.

The Child Labour (Prohibition and Regulation) Bill 1986 was passed in both the Houses of Parliament and was converted into an Act on 234.12.1986. The Employment of Children Act, 1938, was repealed by the Child Labour (Prohibition and Regulation) Act, 1986. Actually, the new Act has intended to extend the scope of the provisions of the old Act, in as much as the old Act was meant for Ports and Railway Establishments in particular, whereas the present enactment is its extension to establishments, which includes shops, commercial establishments, workshops, farms, residential hotels, restaurant etc. Under this Act an 'establishment' means a shop, commercial establishment, workshop, farm, residential hotel, restaurant, eating house, theatre or other place of public amusement of entertainment.

The Regulation of Conditions of Work of Children: The specific sections of the act which regulate conditions of work of children are discussed below:

Section 6: Stipulates that the provisions of this part shall apply to an establishment for the class of establishments in which none of the occupations or processes referred to in Section 3 is carried on.

Section 7: Details and the hours and period of work: it shows that no child shall be required or permitted to work in any establishment in excess of such number of hours as may be described for such establishment or class of establishment. The period of work on each day shall be so fixed that no period shall exceed 3 hours before he has had an interval for rest for at least one hour. The period of work of a child shall be so arranged to include his interval for rest and it shall not be spread over time form 6 hours including one time spent in waiting for work on any day. No child shall be permitted or required to work between 7 p.m. and 8 a.m. or work in any establishment or any day on which he has already been working in another establishment.

Section 8: Stipulates that every child employed in establishment shall be allowed in each week holiday of one whole day, which day shall be specified by the occupier in notice form permanently exhibited in a conspicuous place in the establishment and one day so specified shall not be altered by the occupier more than once in 3 months.

Section 9: Makes provision for furnishing information regarding employment of a child labour to Inspector.

Section 10: As per Section 10 of the Act, if any question arises between an inspector and an occupier as to the age of any child who is employed or is permitted to work by him in an establishment the question shall in the absence of a certificate as to the age of such child granted by the prescribed medical authority be referred by the Inspector for examination to the prescribed medical authority.

Section 11: Makes provision for maintenance of the prescribed register. These shall be maintained by every occupier in respect of children engaged or permitted to work in any establishment; a register to be available for inspection by an Inspector at all times during working hours or when work is being carried on in any such establishment.

Section 12: Makes provision for display of notice in a conspicuous place at the establishment regarding publication of employment of child labour penalties etc. in the local language and in English.

Section 13: The section 13 lays down that Government is required to make rules for the health and safety of the child labour.

Section 14: Provides for penalties for contravention of the provisions of the Act.

Section 15: Makes provision for penalties under the Act even when any person is found guilty and convicted of contravention of any of the provisions mentioned there in:

1. Where any person is found guilty and convicted of contravention of any of the provisions mentioned in sub-section (2), he shall be liable to penalties as provided in sub-section (1) and (2) of Section 14 of this Act and not under the Acts in which those provisions are contained.
2. The provisions referred to sub section (1) are the provisions mentioned under (a) Section 67 of the Factory Act, 1948 (63 of 1948); (b) Section 40 of the Mines Act, 1952 (35 of 1952); (C) Section 109 of the Merchant Shipping Act, 1958 (44 of 1958), and (d) Section 21 of the Motor Transport Workers Act, 1961 (27 of 1961).

Section 16: Lays down that any person who is a police officer, or an inspector, can file a complaint regarding commission of offences. It also lays down the procedure for disposal of the complaints.

Section 17: The appropriate court is empowered to appoint inspectors for securing compliance of the provisions of the Act and any inspector so appointed shall be deemed to be a public servant within the meaning of the Indian Penal Code (45 of 1860).

Section 18: Empowers the appropriate government to make rule for carrying out, the provisions of the Act.

Section 19: Under Section 19, the rules and notification to be laid before Parliament or State Legislature for approval.

Section 20: Lays down that the provisions of this Act shall be in addition to the provisions of the Acts mentioned therein.

Subject to the provisions contained in Section 15, the provisions of this Act and the rules made there under. These provisions shall be in addition to and not in derogation of the provisions of the Factory Act; 1948 (63 of 1943), the Plantation Labour Act 1951, (69 of 1951), and the Mines Act, 1952 (35 of 1952).

Section 21: Empowers the Central Government to remove difficulties which arise in giving effect to the provisions of this Act.

Section 22: Repeals the Employment of Children Act 1938: (1) the Employment of Children Act, 1938 (26 of 1938) is hereby repealed, and (2) Notwithstanding such repeal anything done or any action taken or purported to have been done or taking under the Act so reflected shall in so far as it is not inconsistent with the provisions of this Act be deemed to have been done or taken under the corresponding provisions of this Act.

Section 23: Section 2 of the Minimum Wages Act 1948 has been amended by Section 23, and defines the terms 'Adolescent', 'Adult' and 'Child'.

1. For clause (A) the following clauses shall be substituted, namely—(a) 'Adult' means a person who has completed 18th year of age, (b) 'Adolescent' means a person who has completed his 14 years of age but has not completed his 18 years.
2. After clause (b) the following clauses shall be inserted, namely, (b) 'Child' means a person who has not completed his 14 years of age.

The schedule attached to the Act details the occupations under Part-A and processes under Part-B which includes six categories of occupations and 13 processes. The occupational categories are: (1) Transport of passengers, goods or mails in Railways; (2) Under Packing, cleaning of an ash pit or building operation in the railway premises; (3) Work in a catering establishment at a railway station involving the movement of a vendor or any other employee of the establishment from one platform to another or into out of a moving train; (4) Work relating to the construction of a railway station with any other work where such work in done in close proximity to or between the railway lines; (5) Port Authority within the limits of any Port; and (6) Work relating to selling of crackers and fire works in shops with temporary license.

The processes included are: (1) Bidi-making, (2) Carpet-weaving, (3) Cement manufacture including bagging of cement, (4) Cloth-printing, dyeing and weaving, (5) Manufacture of matches, explosives and fire-works, (6) Mica-cutting and splitting, (7) Shellac manufacture, (8) Soap manufacture, (9) Tanning, (10) Wool cleaning, (11) Building and construction industry, (12) Manufacture of Slate pencils, and (13) Manufacturing process using toxic metal and substances, such as Lead, Mercury, Manganese, Chromium, Cadmium, Benze pesticides and Asbestos.

Committees and Commissions on Child Labour in India

Some of the observations and the findings of various Committees and Commissions which have investigated the conditions of the labour in general and of the child labour in particular in India from time to time.

1. The Royal Commission on Labour, 1929

This Commission which was set up in 1929, observed that there was considerable incidence of child labour in bidi-making and plantation as well as in carpet weaving in Mirzapur district (United Province) and in tanneries in Amritsar district of Punjab. The Commission referred at length to the child labour in plantations where children, accompanied by their parents, lived in tea gardens. Chances of education of these children were almost nil and hence, the Commission recommended that the owners of the tea plantations should contribute towards the establishment of facilities for ensuring their minimum education. The Commission recommended legal prohibition for children below the age of 10 to work and to have an entry of the names of all working children in the wage book. The Commission observed that in many cities a large number of young boys were employed in bidi-making, who worked for long hours and under strict discipline. The Commission recommended that this minimum age for employment should be raised to 14 years.

The Commission effort to prohibit and regulate the employment of children below the minimum age was faced with contrasting issues, such as dislocation and hardship of parents of these children. The Commission recommended that children should not be allowed to work overtime or take the work home and prohibit the pledging or children, observing the economic realities of the time and of child labour. It observed that "Child's right to childhood and even to such education as may be available should make no appeal comparable to its earning capacity".

On the whole, the Commission adopted a conciliatory approach and recommended cooperation between the Government, that local authorities and the employers to develop child welfare centers and clinics for children.

2. Labour Investigation Committee, 1944

The Labour Investigating Committee, popularly known as Rege Committee, observed that child labour declined from the peak of 74,620 (5.3 per cent of total employment) in 1923 to 9,403 (0.5 per cent in 1939), but showed a slight increase during war time. As the data were unreliable, the Committee concluded that "the employment of children (up to 15 years of age) has gone down considerable since the beginning of the century". The child laobur was predominant in bidi-making, carpet-weaving, glass and other small scale industries. The report specially referred its prevalence in the match industry in South India, cement industry in Rajasthan, Spinning industry in Cochin, and carpet-weaving in Kashmir. The Committee recommended that it is not enough to prohibit the employment of children, but it is also essential to adopt simultaneously positive measures to warn them away from industrial employment.

3. National Commission on Labour, 1966

The National Commission on Labour observed that the employment of children is indeed more of an economic problem than anything else. However, denial of opportunity to children for their proper physical development and education was considered a serous issue keeping in view of the larger interest of the society. The Commission recommended fixing of the minimum age for children, fixing working hours of the child labour and making arrangements for work along with informal education for the child labourers.

4. Gurupadaswamy Committee, 1979

The Gurupadaswamy Committee on Child Labour set up in 1979 was an additional evidence of the nation's resolve to initiate concrete policy measures for the protection of working children. The report which was both analytical and comprehensive, dealt at length with the questions, such as the dimensions of child labour, status of legislation and its implementation and welfare and training schemes for the child labour. The report also carried out some enquiries for ascertaining the points of views of workers, employers and the Government on aspects, such as what is child labour, what compels children to work, what are the occupations in which children are employed and why child labour is preferred.

Some of the observations and the recommendations of the Committee are:

1. A multiple policy approach is necessary in dealing with the problems of working children.

2. Child labour is not homogenous groups and, therefore, should be divided among the categories of wage-earners, family workers, apprentices in traditional crafts and children who are both working and going to school.
3. The minimum age for entry into employment should be 15.
4. The existing laws relating to prohibition and regulation, of employment of children should be consolidated into a simple comprehensive one.
5. There should be a minimum educational qualification, say the eighth standard; for entry into any regulated employment.
6. The Government should initiate dialogue with the trade unions for developing institutional framework for collective bargaining in respect of the needs of the working children.
7. The planning Commission should work out the feasibility of removing children below 15 years from the labour market to facilitate the unemployed and able-bodied persons to get job opportunities.
8. The educational policy should have an appropriate curriculum and suitable schedules of vacations and holidays to suit the rural environment. Non-formal education facilities should be arranged in the areas where there are more working children.
9. Crèches/child-care centers should be established at the school premises or at community centers in rural areas so as to encourage girls who have to take care of young siblings in the family, to attend school.
10. Periodical medical check-up should be arranged for child labour and rules should be framed so as to ensure a hygienic working environment.
11. The Apprenticeship Act should be enforced effectively.

12. Systematic efforts should be made to identify hazardous jobs for children and their occupational diseases and treatment.

Child Labour - Policies and Programmes

A number of policies and programmes have been undertaken during the last decade or so, with the basic objective of dealing with the problem of child labourers. The formulation of a National Child Labour Policy, 1987, the setting up of a Task Force on child labour and the ratification of the Convention on the Rights of the Child have all formed a part of this process. The Ministry of Labour formulates coordinates and implements policies and programmes for the welfare of child labour. It provides grants to voluntary organisation which run projects of rehabilitation of child labour through non-formal education, health care and supplementary nutrition. The National Policy on Child Labour was formulated in 1987 which, apart form requiring enforcement of legal provisions to protect the interest of children, envisages focusing of general development programmes for the benefit of child labour and project-based plans of action in areas of high concentration of child labour. Under the project action plan of the policy, National Child Labour Projects (NCLP) have been set up in different areas to rehabilitate child labour. A major activity under the NCLP is the establishment of special schools to provide non-formal education, vocational training, supplementary nutrition, etc., to children withdrawn from employment.

The drive for the elimination of child labour has received further impetus after the announcement of a new programme in 1994 for the rehabilitation of children working in hazardous occupations. Under the programme as estimated two million children are to be withdrawn from employment and put in special schools to enable them to become productive members of the society. India has also been participating in the International Programme on

Elimination of Child Labour (IPEC) of working children covered by the special schools is minuscule compared to the total number of children waiting to be released and rehabilitated. Evidently, the goal cannot be achieved in one stroke. Considering the magnitude of the problem and the paucity of the resources human, material and financial—a sequential, gradual but integrated approach should be adopted. All efforts should be made to convert working children into productive and participated members of the society.

Measures for Eradication of Child Labour

In spite of the efforts made by the Government of India and NGOs, the problem of child labour is still persisting in the economy. In order to sustain high growth of human development of future human capital of the country some stringent measures or policies are essential for the protection of health, literacy, quality of life of child labour.

The following are the important measures for the control and eradication of child labour in the country:

1. Effective implementation of the legislation for the protection of child labour. Minimum level of wages, good working conditions, fixed intervals of work, abolition of hazardous occupation etc. are essential for their protection.
2. Poverty alleviation through different developmental programmes must reach the poorest of the poor. The trickle down effect will rise the standards of living as a result the supply of child labour will be controlled to a large extent.
3. Compulsory education for children below 14 years and universalisation of education for all will combat the problems of reducing the dropouts and increase the retention and enrolment in the schools, which directly reduces the child labour.

4. Good medical and balanced diet for working children should be evolved.
5. Provisions of proper housing facilities with basic amenities will also contribute to the health and growth of children.
6. Research and documentation of the different problems of child labour will focus the attention of the policy-makers, researchers, activities to take steps for the eradication of child labour and it also helps in bringing the National Child Policy for their protection.
7. Strict implementation of family planning and awareness generation on small family size will control the problem.
8. Effective mass media strategies for the control of child labour through the creation of awareness on child rights, usefulness of education for children, good conditions of child work etc. will have impact on the community.
9. Interventions of NGOs for rehabilitation of the child labour by protecting them from neglect, cruelty and exploitations.
10. Incentives to the working children in the form of free meal, rest room, recreation, necessary facilities for those children coming straight from work to schools.
11. Expansion of employment opportunities in the economy, provision of training, skill development, self-employment generation etc. will control the evils of poverty, unemployment low level of living standards and other adverse effects of the poor.

Imapct of Child Labour Earnings on the Level of Living of Households

The Third Section brings out the impact of the child labour earnings on the economic conditions of the households of child labour, association between employment of child labourers and their earnings, factors influencing the magnitude of child labour.

This section has two parts. In the first part, analysis of the impact of child labour earnings on the economic conditions of their households such as income and savings has been done. In the second part of this section, association between employment of child labourers and their earnings, factors influencing the magnitude of child labour.

Part – 1

Distribution of Child Labourers based on the Contribution to their Family Income

Family being the basic unit, earning members contribute to the family fund so that at least the basic needs of all family members including non-earning members is satisfied. The distribution of the child labourers in terms of their contribution to their family income is presented in Table 6.15.

Table 6.15
Distribution of Child Labourers based on the Contribution to their Family Income

Sl. No.	*Range of Per cent contribution to the total income of the family*	*Number of contributors*	*Percentage*
1.	Up to 10	13	4.33
2.	11 to 20	21	7.00
3.	21 to 50	47	15.67
4.	51 to 100	219	73.00
	Total	300	100.00

Source: Computed form Survey Data

Table 6.15 shows that a good number of children that is 219 (73 per cent), gave 51 to 100 per cent of their monthly earnings, 47 (15.67 per cent) have given between 21 and 50 per cent, 21 (7 per cent) between 11 and 20 per cent and 13 (4.33 per cent) gave only 10 per cent of their monthly earnings to the total income of their families.

This reveals that the majority of the working children in the agriculture labour. They are socially as well as economically poor families and they supplemented the family earnings to a great extent. The poor economic conditions force children to take up jobs at an early age for contributing to the family income.

Average Annual Income of the Housholds Before and After the Contribution of Child Labourers

The average annual income of the households before and after the contribution of child labourers is presented Table 6.16.

Table 6.16
Average Annual Income of the Housholds Before and After the Contribution of Child Labourers

Sl. No.	Category	Average Annual Income (in Rs.)
1.	Before contribution of Child Labourers	14,863.67 (77.59)*
2.	Contribution of Child Labourers	4,293.97 (22.41)**
3.	After Contribution of Child Labourers	19,157.64 (100.00)

Source: Computed from Survey Data.

Note: * The percentage average income of the households without the contribution of child labour to average annual income of households.

** The percentage of contribution of child labourer's income to the average income of households.

It is evident from Table 6.16 that the average income of the respondents from different occupations is 4,293.97 (22.41 per cent) and the average income of the households without the contribution of child labourers is Rs. 14,863.67 (77.59 per cent). Taking the contribution of child labourers into consideration, the average income of the households is raised to 19,157.64. The table further reveals that out of the average income of the households after the contribution of child labourers, the average income of child labour constituted 22.41 per cent. This infers that nearly one fourth of the households income is contributed by child labour. Here, it is very difficult to maintain the family in the prevailing standard of living without contribution of child labour. From this table it may be inferred that the contribution of child labour in terms of money per year on an average is sum of Rs. 4,293.87. The additional source of income to the households may be explored. The increase in the income of the households could help the parents in sending their children to schools.

In Table 6.17, it is shown that within the brackets of annual household income of Rs. 11,001 to Rs. 20,000, there are 118 (39.33 per cent) households before the contribution of child labourers which increased to 149 (49.67 per cent) after the contribution of child labourers. The number of families having household income below Rs. 11,000 has decreased from 116 to 49 after the contribution of child labourers.

Income Distribution of Households of Child Labourers Before and After the Contribution of Child Labourers

Table 6.17 shows the income-wise distribution of households of child labour before and after the contribution of child labour.

Table 6.17
Income Distribution of Households of Child Labourers Before and After the Contribution of Child Labourers

Sources	*Below Rs. 11,000*	*Rs. 11,001- Rs. 20,000*	*Rs. 20,001- 30,000*	*Above Rs. 30,000*	*Total*
Before Contribution of Child Labour	116 (38.67)	118 (39.33)	47 (15.67)	19 (6.33)	300 (100)
After Contribution of Child Labour	49 (16.33)	149 (49.67)	74 (24.67)	28 (9.33)	300 (100)

Source: Computed from Survey Data.

In the range of annual income between Rs. 20,001 and Rs. 30,000, there are 47 households before contribution from the child labourers, but this has been increased to 74 after their contribution, the percentage of households being changed from 15.67 to 24.67. This means that household income of 27 respondents crossed Rs. 20,001 to Rs. 30,000 after the contribution of child labourers.

Out of 300 households, 19 have an annual income above Rs. 30,000 before the contribution of child labourers, which has increased to 28; in terms of percentage, the increase is from 6.33 to 9.33. This implies that the income of nine households has crossed Rs. 30,000 after the contribution of child labourers.

This table indicates that the employment of child labourers has helped to enhance the financial position of the households, so that some families have crossed the poverty line. This can be the argument for the continuance of the child labourers.

In the lowest brackets of income below Rs. 11,000 (poverty line) per annum, there are 116 (38.67 per cent) households before the contribution of child laborers, but it declined to 49 (16.33 per cent) after their contribution. This means that out of 116 households who were below the poverty line before the contribution of child labourers, about 67 (116-49) have crossed the poverty line due to the wage earnings of child labourers. This comes to 22.33 per cent of the total 300 households.

Though the wage earnings of the children have helped about 67 households to cross the poverty line, it cannot be a sound argument for the employment of child labourers is justifiable.

This further implies that if the income from child labour is excluded from the household income, the percentage of households below the poverty line rose from 16.33 to 38.67. Thus nearly one-fourth of the households seem to have crossed the poverty line by supplementing their income through the child labour.

A comparison of the percentage of the total income of the households after the contribution of child labourers clearly indicates a positive impact on the annual income of the households of the child labourers.

Analysis of Percentage Share of Children's Contribution to the Family Income

The main objective of this analysis is to find out whether the contribution children to the family budget is substantial or not and also to find out whether the families of the working children can maintain themselves without the contribution of the child labourers to the family budget. Hence, it is necessary to test the validity of the hypothesis. Forthis, the proportional Analysis under 'Z' test* is used, since n>30.

Results and Discussion

The 'Z' test results are tabulated in Table 6.18. It is observed that the calculated value of 'Z' is 16.56 which is greater than the table value of 'Z' (=2.58) at 1 per cent level of significance. Thus it means that there is a significant difference between the proportional average contributions of the parents and the children to the family income.

Table 6.18
Percentage Contribution to the Family Income

Source of Variation	*Calculated Value of 'Z'*	*Table Value of 'Z' at 5% level*	*Table Value of 'Z' at 1% level*
P.A.C-P.C.C.	16.56*	1.96	2.58

Source: Computed from Survey Data.
Note : P.A.C. – Proportion of Adult's Contribution
P.C.C. – Proportion of Children's Contribution
* Significant at 1 per cent level.

Hence, one can accept the hypothesis that income has increased more after the contributions of child labourers. Hence, it is concluded that the contributions of the children's earnings play a significant role in the family budget and it has substantially increased the income of the families of the children and the families may not maintain their present standard without the contributions of the working children.

Analysis of Inequality in the Distribution of Income Before and After the Contribution of Child Labourers

The main objective of this analysis is to make a comparison of the inequality of income distribution before and after the contribution of child labourers. There are various methods available for measuring inequalities in income distribution. In this study, the Lorenz Curve and Gini Coefficient Ratio are used to test the inequality of income before and the contribution of child labourers.

Lorenz Curve

The Lorenz Curve Express graphically the size distribution of income described in percentage. It is obtained by plotting the cumulative percentage of households from the poorest to the richest along the horizontal axis and the cumulative percentage of income along the vertical axis. The straight line connecting the two corners of the figure is known as the line of equal distribution. The Lorenz Curve would coincide with the line of equal distribution when there is perfect equality of income, whereas for perfect inequality of income, the curve would coincide with the horizontal axis and the right hand vertical axis of the graph. The greater its concavity, the greater is the inequality of income and vice versa.

Hence, this technique reveals that a higher. Gini ratio denotes a higher inequality of income and vice versa. It is obvious, therefore, that any Lorenz Curve will be below the diagonal line. This is observed in Figure.

The figure shows that the concavity is less after. This contribution of child labourers than before their contribution.

Figure 6.1
Lorenz Curue For Inequality of Income

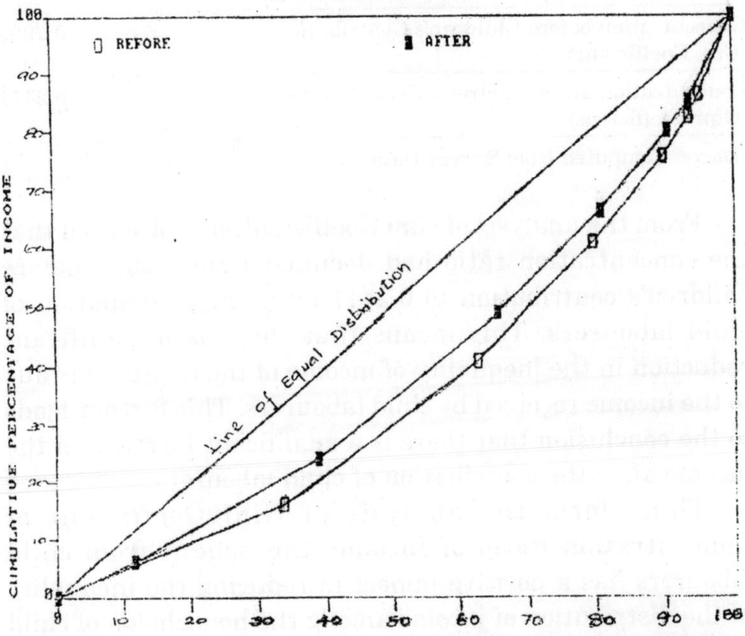

This means that there is a significant reduction in the inequality of income of the households due to the contribution of child labourers.

Gini Coefficient

Gini Coefficient is another simple and useful device to measure the concentration of income distribution. It is used because of its relation with Lorenz Curve. Gini Coefficient is equal to the ratio of the area circumscribed by the Lorenz Curve and the diagonal line of equal distribution to the total area of the triangle below the diagonal.

Result and Discussion

The concentration of income ratio before and after contribution of child labour is shown in Table 6.19.

Table 6.19
Gini Coefficient Before and After the Contribution of Child Labourers

Concentration before Children's Contribution (Gini Coefficient)	0.2962
Concentration after Children's Contribution (Gini Coefficient)	0.2411

Source: Computed from Survey Data.

From the analysis of Gini Coefficient, it is observed that the concentration ratio had declined form 0.2962 before children's contribution to 0.2411 after the contribution of child labourers. This means that there is a significant reduction in the inequality of income of the households due to the income received by child labourers. This further leads to the conclusion that there is a significant increase in the income after the contribution of child labourers.

Thus, form the analysis of Gini Coefficient of Concentration Ratio of Income, the benefit from child labourers has a positive impact in reducing the inequality in the distribution of income among the households of child labourers.

Section - III

Analysis of the Intensity of Poverty of the Households of the Working Children Before and after the Contribution of Child Labourers

The purpose of this analysis is to measure and compare the intensity of poverty of the households of the working children before and after the contribution of child labourers. Sen's Index of Poverty is used to measure the intensity of poverty.

Result and Discussion

Table 6.20 shows Sen's Index of poverty with its components, namely,

- The Head-Count Ratio,

- The Income-Gap Ratio, and
- Gini Coefficient of concentration in respect of households falling below the poverty line before and after the contribution of child labourers.

Table 6.20
Distibution of Head-Count Ratio, Income Gap Ratio, Gini Coefficient of Concentration among the Poor and Sen's Poverty Index for both Before and After the Contribution of Child Labourers

	Head Count Ratio (H)	*Income Gap Ratio (I)*	*Gini Coefficient of Concentration (G)*	*Sen's Index of Poverty (P)*
Before child labourers' contribution	0.3867	0.3139	0.2638	0.1914
After child labourers' contribution	0.1633	0.2041	0.1067	0.0472

Source: Computed from Survey Data.

Table 6.21
Percentage Change in the Valves of H, I, G, and P

Source	*Head Count Ratio (H)*	*Income Gap Ratio (I)*	*Gini Coefficient of Concentration (G)*	*Sen's Index of Poverty (P)*
BCCL ACCL	-22.34	-10.98	-15.71	-14.42

Source: Computed from survey Data.
Note: BCCL – Before Contribution of Child Labourers.
ACCL – After Contribution of Child Labourers.

Table 6.21 shows the change in the percentage of the values of the different components of the index of poverty, namely, the Head-Count Ratio (H), the Income Gap Ratio (I), Gini Coefficient (G) and Sen's Index of Poverty (P) between the two periods.

It is inferred from Table 2.6 and 2.7 that the Head-Count Ratio, that is the percentage of people living below the poverty line had decreased by 22.34 per cent due to the contribution of child labourers.

The analysis of the Income Gap Ratio shows that is reduced by 10.98 per cent. Gini Coefficient of Concentration has also marked a decreasing rate. The Concentration Ratio decreases by 15.71 per cent. This that there is a reduction in the inequality of the distribution of income among households of child labourers to the extent of 15.71 per cent.

Sen's Index of poverty has shown that there is a considerable reduction in the intensity of poverty among the people living below the poverty line. The intensity of poverty has been reduced by 14.42 per cent due to the contribution of child labourers.

Average Annual Savings of the Households Before and After the Contribution of Child Labourers

From Table 6.22, it is obvious that before the contribution of child labourers the average annual savings of households is Rs. 1,150.40 and after that their contribution it is Rs.1,678.43. There is an increase of 45.90 per cent in the average of annual savings before their contribution. Thus, the impact of child earnings on the savings of their households is very significant.

The impact of child labour earnings on the savings of the households is presented in Table 6.22.

Table 6.22
Average Annual Savings of the Households Before and After the Contribution of Child Labourers

(In Rs.)

Sl. No.	*Category*	*Average Annual Savings*	*Increasing in Savings*
1.	BCCL	1,150.40	—
2.	ACCL	1,678.43	45.90

Source: Computed from Survey Data.
Note: BCCL – Before Contribution of Child Labourers.
ACCL – After Contribution of Child labourers.

Section – IV

Analysis of the Impact of Child Labourer on Savings of Households

The main objective of this part of analysis is to find out whether the employment of has any impact on the household savings. This is done by calculating the household income before and after the contribution of child labourers. The simple linear functions of savings are given in Table 6.23.

Table 6.23
Simple Linear Functions of Savings
(Y= a + bx)

Sl.No.	*Category*	*Coefficient of X (b)*
1.	BCCL	0.3895
2.	ACCL	0.5082

Source: Computed from Survey Data.
Note: BCCL – Before Contribution of Child Laborers.
ACCL – After Contribution of Child Labourers.

The marginal propensity to save is given by 'b', coefficient of '*x*' in absolute figures. The marginal propensity to save before contribution of child labourers is 0.3895, where after their contribution it is 0.5082. Thus, marginal propensity to save after contribution of child labourers is greater than before their contribution to the family income.

Part–II

Association between Employment of Child Labourers and their Earnings

In this part, the association between employment of child labourers and their earnings is tested with the Chi-Square (*x*2).

The Age of Child Labourers is associated with the Earnings of Child Labourers

The main objective of this part of analysis is to find whether the age of the children is associated their earnings or not.

Table 6.24
The Age of Children and their Earnings

Source of Variance	*Calculated Value Of Chi-Square*	*Table Value of Chi-Square at 1% level*
ECL – ACL	13.04	6.63

Source: Computed from Survey Data.
Note: ECL - Earnings of Child Labourers.
ACL - Age of Child Labourers.

From the Table, it is observed that the calculated value of $x2$ is 13.04 which is greater than the table value $x2$ (= 6.63) at 1 per cent level of significance. Hence, one can say that earnings of child labourers are associated with their age.

The Size of the Family is associated with the Earnings of Child Labourers

Similar technique ($x2$ test) is adopted to find whether the size of the family is, associated with the earnings of child labourers.

Table 6.25
The Size of the Family and the Earnings of Child Labourers

Source of Variance	*Calculated Value of Chi-Square*	*Table Value of Chi - Square at 1% level*
ACL - SF	62.21	6.63

Source: Computed from Survey Data.
Note: ACL - Earnings of Child Labourers.
SF - Size of the Family.

Since it is observed from Table 6.25 that the calculated value of $x2$ is 62.21 which is greater than the table value of ($x2$ = 6.63) at 1 per cent level of significance, it is concluded that the size of the family is associated with the earnings of the child labourers.

Income of Parents is associated with the Earnings of Child Labourers

The result of the $x2$ test which is used to find whether the income of parents is associated with the earnings of child labourers is presented in Table 6.26.

Table 6.26
Income of Parents and Earnings of Child Labourers

Source of Variance	*Calculated Value of Chi-Square*	*Table Value of Chi-Square at 1% level*
ACL - IP	16.11	6.63

Source: Computed from Survey Data.
Note: ACL – Earnings of Child Labour.
IP – Income of Parents.

It is observed from the table that the calculated value of x2 is 16.11 which is greater than the table value of x2 (=6.63) at 1 per cent level of significance. This implies that the income of parents is associated with the earnings of child labourers.

Employment Function

An attempt is made to study the influence of various factors on the employment of child labourers in terms of number of hours employed per annum. In this function, employment of hours of work done by child labourers per annum (y) is the dependent variable and it is related to a set of independent variables, such as family size (Xl), household income in rupees per annum (X2) and the children's wage earnings in rupees per annum (X3).

Employment Function of Male Child Labourers

The result of the estimated Multiple Regression Model covering 72 male child labourers' households are presented in Table 6.27.

The estimated equation for male child labourers' households shows a good fit with a high explanatory power as shown by the value of R^2 at 0.96. Thus, the entire three explanatory variables explain 96 per cent of variation in employment of child labourers.

Employment of male child labourers' to be more sensitive to the size of the family. The calculated coefficient is 306.7865 which is significant at 1 per cent level.

Table 6.27
Employment Function of Male Child Labourers' Households
(Y = a0 + a1x1 + a2x2+a3x3+U)

Explanatory Variable	*Regression Coefficients*	*'t' value*
Intercept	765.5473*	4.885
Family Size (Xl)	306.7865*	11.936
Households Income (X2)	0.0022	0.610
Children's Wage Earnings (X3)	0.2597	1.416
R^2	0.9598	
F-Value	533.1295	
N = 72		

Source: Computed from Survey Data.
Note: *Significant at 1 per cent level.

Even though household income is an important determinant of employment in general, it is insignificant in the cause of male child labourers. Again the negative sign of the coefficient implies that as household income falls, the employment of children is increased. Since child labourers provide supplementary income to their households, as household income falls, more and more hours of work is done by child labourers.

The variable, children's wage earnings is found to have no significant influence of the employment of the employment of male child labourers.

Employment Function of Female Child Labourers' Households

Table 6.28 illustrates the result of the estimated Multiple Regression Model covering 228 female child labourers' households.

Table 6.28 shows that all the three explanatory variables explain 98 per cent variation in the employment of female working children since the calculated R^2 value is 0.98.

The estimated value of the regression coefficient for family size is 252.7105 and it is significant at 1 per cent level. It comes first in 'order of importance' among the three factors. Therefore, the size of the family has a positive and significant influence on the employment of female child labourers.

Table 6.28
Employment Function of Female Child Labourers' Households
(Y = a0 + alxl + a2x2 + a3x3 + U)

Explanatory Variable	*Regression Coefficients*	*'t' value*
Intercept	992.1411*	19.920
Family Size (Xl)	252.7105*	30.709
Households Income (X2)	-0.0032*	-2.390*
Children's Wage Earnings (X3)	0.0437*	6.104
R^2	0.9800	
F-Value	3491.5935	
N = 228		

Note: *Significant at 1 per cent level.

Further, it is evident that the household income has negatively contributed to the employment of female children and it is significant at 1 per cent level. Hence, household income is negatively and significantly influencing the employment of female children of the selected households.

The estimated value of the regression coefficient for female children's wage earnings is 0.0437 and it is significant at 1 per cent level. Hence, wage earnings of female children are positively related to their employment.

Employment Function of both Male and Female Child Labourers' Households

The result of the estimated Multiple Regression Model for 300 child labourers' households consisting of 72 male and 228 female child labourers are depicted in Table 6.29.

The equation presented in Table 6.29 related to all the child labourers under the study has a high explanatory power as evident from the very high values of the coefficient of determination (R^2 = 0.97).

Table 6.29
Employment Function of both Male and Female Child Labourers' Households
(Y = a0 + a1x1 + a2x2 + a3x3 + U)

Explanatory Variable	*Regression Coefficients*	*'t' value*
Intercept	974.2899*	18.719
Family Size (Xl)	258.6931*	30.034
Households Income (X2)	-0.0038	-2.824
Children's Wage Earnings (X3)	0.0427*	5.910
R^2	0.9700	
F-Value	3386.0946	
N = 300		

Note: * Significant at 1 per cent level.

The results show that all the three variables, namely, size of the family, household income and children's wage earnings are the major determinants of child employment in terms of hours of work done per annum. The coefficients of these variables are highly significant at 1 per cent level as their 't' values are 30.034, –2.824 and 5.910 respectively. Since the size of the family has a positive and significant influence on the employment of child labourers, the hypothesis that "higher the family size. Higher will be employment of children, lower the family size, less will be the employment of children" has been proved to be correct.

The estimated value of the regression coefficient of children's for children's wage earnings has a positive and significant influence on employment of working children. Hence, the hypothesis that "higher the children's" wage earnings, the higher will be their working hours and vice versa has been proved to be correct.

The negative sign of the coefficient of the variable households' income implies that there is inverse relationship between the households' income and employment of child labourers. Hence, the hypotheses that "lower the household's income, the higher will be the employment of children, higher the household's income, the lower will be the employment of children" is strongly supported. This implies that when the income of the households is higher, there would be lesser tendency in the family to send the children to work.

Chapter - 7

CONCLUSION AND RECOMMENDATIONS

This chapter is presents the summary, findings and conclusions and also the policy recommendations to be implemented to solve the problem of child labour in Kurnool district of Andhra Pradesh.

Kumool district had the dubious distinction of having the largest number of child labour, i.e. 10,55,407 (According to NCLP Survey 2001). There is lot of child labour families migrated from surrounding districts and other states like Bangalore, Mumbai and Chennai etc. Migration of families from rural areas in order to earn their bread, working children, children of very poor parents, abandoned, delinquents, orphans and maladjusted are found in Kurnool district of Andhra Pradesh. Migrated parents who themselves never had an opportunity to get education, could not send their children to school, being ignorant of the value of education themselves, the parents were not in a position to provide guidance and encouragement for their children's education. This contributed to reinforcing the cycle of ignorance, illiteracy, poverty and child labour. Children working in almost all sectors, like Agriculture, Cattle grazing, Lime line, Stone quarries, Shepherds, Livestock, Domestic works, Migrated working in construction, Auto garage, Cycle shops, Petty shops, etc., and they have been deprived of their basic needs and exploited. So, a case study will be undertaken in Kurnool district of Andhra Pradesh in order to examine the miserable conditions of Child Labour.

Child labour is not restricted with in a particular place, particular district, and particular country. It is to be considered as a global problem. Children are always taken as additional helpers for domestic, agricultural or industrial work. The parents send their children to work rather than to schools because their contribution will help to maintain their families in the present standard of living. Children's employed all possible sectors is preferred because of the following reasons:

- They work less remuneration than adult labourers.
- They are more flexible mentally as well as physically and can moulded and pressurised easily into the exploitative tactics of the employers.
- Child labour is not only very cheap to the employers, but also trouble-free since they can't organize agitations by themselves.
- Children cannot demand any overtime, nor the medical and other similar benefits.
- Employers find children more amenable to discipline and control.

The employment is a curse not only for the child but also for the society as a whole. Moreover, socio-economic reasons such as poverty and backwardness, illiteracy etc. force children into the workforce. The child, who goes to work forfeits not only his childhood, but also fair chance to leave behind his gloomy past. He losses his chance to receive education and rise his status in life. Article 24 of the Constitution of India provides that no child below the age of 14 years shall be employed to work in any factory or mine to be engaged in any hazardous employment. Article 45 says, "The state shall endeavour to provide, within a period of ten years from the commencement of this Constitution, for free and compulsory education for all children until they complete age of fourteen years." It is unfortunate that even after 56 years of Independence we would not succeed.

Child labour in the Kurnool district has been discussed in the fifth chapter. After the objectives of the study are also explained. The objectives of the present study are:

1. To identify the socio-economic factors which led to the perpetuation of child labour in Kurnool district.
2. To present the spatial and social dimensions of child labour.
3. To assess the sectoral dimensions.
4. To record the wage pattern of child labour and due to estimate the proportion of their contribution to their family income.
5. To elicit the awareness of different Child Labour Rehabilitation and Regulatory programmes implemented by the State and Central Governments.
6. To suggest the measures which have a regulatory effect on the existence of child labour.

Based on the objectives, a few hypotheses have been framed along with the methodology and statistical tools for testing them, significance of the study and relevance of the study are also given.

The six chapters which formed the basis of Research study are: (1) Human Resource and Child Labour (2) Child Labour: An overview (3) Child Labour: The Global Situation (4) Child Labour in India (5) Economic Role of Children in India and Its States (6) Child Labour: Its Spatial, Social and Occupational Dimentions (7) Conclusion and Recommendations.

Findings and Conclusions

The following are the major findings and conclusions drawn from the analysis of the study.

One of the findings of the study is that out of the 300 child labourers. The ratio between girls and boys is 31.17: 1. Out of 300 sample respondents, 228 (76 per cent) are girls and 72 (24 per cent) are boys. The causes for the employment of more number of female child labourers is the preference by employers to female children. Another reason, girls children are not treated on par with male children. Further, it is found that in almost all the families of the working girls, girls' education is very much neglected compared to boys' education. This does not seen to be a good trend. This is to be corrected.

In the rural areas where the cotton field cultivation is high, the parents of the child labourers prefer the education of the male children to the education of female children. This is a clear case of discrimination against female children by their own parents without knowing that female children also deserve to get education on the basis of their ability and desire to study. The denial of education to girl children amounts to the suppression of their opportunities and spoiling their future.

It is found that the mean earning of the working children (Rs. 4,293.97 per annum) is one-third of the mean earnings of adults (Rs. 14,863.67 per annum). Thus, the contribution of child labourers to their families is sizeable, that is, in total an average of 22 per cent of the total family income is contributed by the children which has substantially increased the income level of the households of the working children. Further, the families will experience difficulty in maintaining their present standard of living without the contribution of child labourers. From the analysis, it is observed that the Gini Ratio had declined from 0.2962 before children's contribution to 0.2411 after their contribution. This implies that there is a significant reduction in the inequality of income of the households of child labourers. Hence, the employment of child labour increases the household income.

It is found that, out of 300 families, 116 families (38.67 per cent) were living below the poverty line prior to the contribution of child labourers. The number declined to 49 (16.33 per cent) after the contribution of the child labourers. This means that out of 116 households who were below poverty line before contribution of child labourers, about 67 (116-49) have crossed the poverty line because of the wage earnings of child labourers. This amounts to 22.33 per cent of the total 300 households. This further implies that if the income from child labour is excluded from the household income, the percentage of households below the poverty line would be 38.67. Thus, nearly one-fourth of the households of the study area seems to have crossed the poverty line by supplementing their income through the child labourers. The intensity of poverty has been reduced by 14.42 per cent because of the contribution of child labourers.

The study able to establish that the savings level was found to be enhanced in all the families of the working children by the contribution of the working children. The marginal propensity to save by the households before contribution of child labourers is 0.3895, whereas after their contribution it is 0.5082.

The study also establish that the size of the family, income of parents and employment of working children are associated with the earnings of child labour.

Here, the family members increases, the employment of working children trends to increase which clearly shows that economic hardships must have compelled the parents to send their children to work to supplement the household income.

The children's wage earnings have a positive and significant influence on the employment of working children.

Household income and employment of children are found to be negatively related. It is clear that lower income of the parents, higher the employment of children. When the income of the parents of the child labourers goes up, the parents' inclination to send them to work in the cotton field.

Policy Recommendations

Based on the findings of the study, the following constructive and practicable suggestions are provided and recommended to minimise the employment of child labour in Kurnool district of Andhra Pradesh.

(1) Various seminars are being held, resolutions passed and plan of action drawn up on the protection of children, yet not much could have been done about child protection and the problems grows out proportion day by day. So, child laws have to be radically re-thought and re-written from the perspective of rights of the child in terms of policy and accountability.

(2) If child labour is banned without any alternative sources of income, there will be fictions in the family and the child may be forced to beg, pickpocket or go unemployed. In the absence of possible alternatives, the abolition of child labour is likely to aggravate rather than mitigate their misery and hardship. Hence, to minimise the magnitude of the child labour at present and to abolish it completely in the years to come, each child labour family should be provided with minimum income by making employment available to the men and women who are ready to work. This would be possible when more employment opportunities are created for the adults through effective enforcement of all the existing antipoverty programmes like, Swarnajayanthi Gram Swarozgar Yojana (SGSY), Self-Help Groups (SHGs), Sampoorna Grameen Rozgar Yojana (SGRY), Society for Elimination of Rural Poverty (SERP), Training for Rural Youth for Self-Employment (TRYSEM), Jawahar Rozgar Yojana (JRY), and Prime Minister Rozgar Yojana (PMRY) with a positive approach and with a sense of

dedication to help the families of child labourers. Unless poverty is eradicated, no legal restriction will solve the problem of child labour. The programmes launched by the Government render little help, for the maximum amount allotted for these schemes are squandered away by the influential people who deal with these schemes. The Government spends thousands of crores in 'poverty alleviation programmes.' The bad situation is that only a few paise of each rupee spent, reaches the targeted groups. Effective measures are to be taken to see that the targeted groups get the benefits of the poverty alleviation programmes due to them.

(3) Failure in education often leads the children being sent to work instead of schooling. Direct correlation exists between literacy rate and work participation rates of children. Hence, universal primary education to all children should be made compulsory in the study area to eliminate child labour. Hence, the researcher strongly feels that unless primary education is made compulsory, it is not possible to eradicate child labour. Further, a committee comprising Headmasters and Village Leaders should be constituted to see that the children are not made to drop out from the school till they attain 14 years of age. Necessary economic assistance should be provided to the economically backward classes.

(4) Teachers are provided the right atmosphere and have the ability to motivate, half the battle of getting children in to schools in won. Teachers themselves need to be resourceful, well-educated and highly motivated. Therefore, teachers who do good work must be honoured and encouraged with awards and certificates of merit. A community that respects teachers will see their children making progress.

(5) Adult literacy programme is felt as essential for creation of awareness among adults about negative impact of child

labour. Though large family size is identified as one of the causes of child labour, there is a myth among the people that family planning operation will disable a person to do, hard work after family planning operation. There is a mental stigma among people on family planning. It is suggested that there is need for educating people on health aspects and family welfare.

(6) Social mobilisation and capacity building: (1) Organisation and social mobilisation of people and all other stakeholders towards elimination of child labour should be a key strategy under RD Programmes, (2) Training of PRI Representatives should include training on the issue of rural child labour, (3) All training institutions should include training on the issue of child labour, (4) There should be convergence of all line departments based on a time bound common action plan for elimination of child labour in the blocks identified with high incidence of child labour.

Certain indicators to assess the improvement of children's lives should be developed while assessing the impact of these programmes. Various departments dealing with social sector development should include indicator-showing decline of child labour.

REFERENCES

Shukal K. & Ali S. 2000, Encyclopedia of Child Labour, Priorities for 21st Century, (1st Volume).

Dak, T.M.K. 2002, Child Labour in India, New Delhi, Serial Publications.

http://www.cdp-hrc.uottawa.ca/publicat/bu13211.html

Daman Ahuja, The Economic of Nimble Fingers-A Myth: Social Welfare, ARY-1996 (pp. 23).

Shibani Dasgupta, Child Labour in India and the World. Monthly Public Opinion Survey, January, 1997 (pp. 17).

Sukla, C.K. & Ali. S, Encyclopedia of Child Labour: Priorities for 21st Century (3rd Volume).

Giri, V.V., Labour Problems in Indian Industry, Asia Publishing House, Bombay, 1972.

Op.cit.

Bhowmik, Sharit K. 'Plantation Labour Act and Child Labour' in Economic and Political Weekly. Vol. XXVII. No. 42, 17 October 1992.

Gore, M.S., 'Opening Address' in Usha Naidu and Kamini R. Kapadia (eds), Child Labour and Health: Problems and Prospects (Bombay: Tata Institute of Social Sciences) 1985.

Marla, Sarma, 'Bonded Labour in Medak District (A.P.)' in NLI Bulletin, Vol. 3, No.10, October 1977.

Marx, Karl, Capital Volume I. Introduced by Ernest Mandle (The Pelican Marx Library, Penguin Books in Association with New Left Review), 1967 & 1982.

Naik, J.P. Equality, Quality and Quantity: The Elusive Triangle in Indian Education (New Delhi: Allied Publishers Private Limited) 1975a.

Naik, J.P. Policy and Performance in Indian Education 1947-74, Dr. K.G. Saividian Memorial Trust, Jaminanagar, New Delhi (New Delhi: Orient Longman) 1975b.

Naik, J.P. The Education Commission and After (New Delhi: Allied Publishers Private Limited), 1982.

Parmegoiani, Luigi, Encyclopedia of Occupational Health and Safety, Third (revised edition), Vol. 2 (Geneva; International Labour Organisation) 1983.

Sudha, B.G. and Smita Tewari, 'Child Labour in Rural Areas: Some Factors in Kurukshetra', Vol. XXXIII, No. 7, April 1985.

NLI Rural Wing, 'The Dark World of Jeeta Gadus' in NLI Bulletin. Vol. 3, No. 12, 1977.

Government of India, Report of the National Commission on Labour, 1969, (pp 386).

Joseph Gathia, The Challenge of Child Labour in Rural India policy response, Paper presented to the National Seminar on Mainstreaming Child Labour into Rural Development Programmes, NIRD, Hyderabad, between April 28 and 30, 2003.

Government of India (1979), Report of the Committees on Child Labour, New Delhi.

Ibid. (1933) The Children (Pledging Labour) Act.

Ibid. (1938) The Employment of Children Act.

Ministry of Labour, Government of India, 1995, Children and Work.

The Child Labour Act 1986, Madras, Madras Book Agency.

Indira Hirway, Jacqui Cottyn and Puskar Pandya (Eds). 1991.

Participatory Learning and Action Towards Elimination of Child Labour in Rural Areas, ILO-IPEC Sponsored Project, Center for Social Development, National Institute of Rural Development, Hyderabad, 2002.

ILO (1997), Year Book of Statistics.

ILO (1999).

Smith Kothari, Op.cit: 1202.

Kothari, C.R. 1989, Research Methodology: New Delhi: Wiley Eastern Limited: 298.

Elhane, D.N. 1973, Fundamentals of Statistics. Allahabad: Kitab Mahal: 228-229.

Grewal, P.S. 1987, Numerical Methods of Statistical Analysis, Jalandhar: Sterling Publishers Pvt. Ltd: 290.

Sen, A.K. 1976, Poverty: An Ordinal Approach to Measurement Econometric 44 (2): 219-231.

Gupta, S.C. 1987, Fundamentals of Statistics, Bombay: Himalaya Publishing House: 1168.

Gupta, S.P. 1987, Statistical Methods, New Delhi: Sultan Chand & Sons: 11.7.

Kothari, C.R. 1984, Quantitative Techniques. New Delhi: Vikas Publishing House Pvt. Ltd: 249.

Project Director, National Child Labour Project, Kurnool.

Vidyasagar, R. Suman Chandra, K. 2002, Training Manual on Child Labour: Child Labour Cell, Center for Social Development, National Institute of Rural Development, Hyderabad. p. 5.

Shah, P.M. International Child Health: A Digest of Current Information. Vol. VII, No. 4, October, 1996.

Ibid 1948, Factories Act.

Govt. of India 1948, Minimum Wage Act.

Kulusreshtha, J.C. 1978, Child Labour in India, Ashish Publishing House, New Delhi.

Pramila H. Bhargava, 2003. The Elimination Child Labour Whose Responsibility? New Delhi: Sage Publications.

Anandharajkumar, P. Child Labour: Issues & Solutions, Kurukshetra, Vol. 47, No. 10, July 1999.

Venkatanarayana, M. "Educational Deprivation of Children in Rural Andhra Pradesh: Causes and Consequences" Paper presented to the National Seminar on Mainstreaming Child Labour into Rural Development Programmes, NIRD, Hyderabad, between April 28 and 30, 2003.

Gokhale
college